Prayer and Discipleship

FOR NEW CHRISTIANS

Copyright 2025

Scripture marked CSB is from The Christian Standard Bible. Copyright © 2017 by Holman Bible Publishers. Used by permission. Christian Standard Bible®, and CSB® are federally registered trademarks of Holman Bible Publishers, all rights reserved.

Scripture marked ESV are taken from The ESV® Bible (The Holy Bible, English Standard Version®). ESV® Text Edition: 2016. Copyright © 2001 by Crossway, a publishing ministry of Good News Publishers. The ESV® text has been reproduced in cooperation with and by permission of Good News Publishers. Unauthorized reproduction of this publication is prohibited. All rights reserved.

Scripture marked KJV is from the King James version, public domain.

Scripture marked MEV is taken from the Modern English Version. Copyright © 2014 by Military Bible Association. Used by permission. All rights reserved.

Scripture marked NCV is taken from the New Century Version®. Copyright © 2005 by Thomas Nelson. Used by permission. All rights reserved.

Scripture marked NIV THE HOLY BIBLE, NEW INTERNATIONAL VERSION®, NIV® Copyright © 1973, 1978, 1984, 2011 by Biblica, Inc.® Used by permission. All rights reserved worldwide.

Scripture marked NIRV is taken from the Holy Bible, NEW INTERNATIONAL READER'S VERSION ®. Copyright © 1996, 1998 Biblica. All rights reserved throughout the world. Used by permission of Biblica.

Scripture marked NKJV is taken from the New King James Version®. Copyright © 1982 by Thomas Nelson. Used by permission. All rights reserved.

Scripture quotations marked NLV are taken from the New Life Version, copyright © 1969 and 2003. Used by permission of Barbour Publishing, Inc., Uhrichsville, Ohio 44683. All rights reserved.

Scripture marked VOICE is taken from The Voice™. Copyright © 2008 by Ecclesia Bible Society. Used by permission. All rights reserved.

Prayer and Discipleship for New Christians

Copyright © 2025 Kathleen Vergers

Published by Sand Pearl Press

All rights reserved. No part of this publication may be reproduced, stored in a retrieval system, or transmitted in any form or by any means—electronic, mechanical, photocopying, recording, or otherwise—without the prior written permission of the publisher, except in the case of brief quotations used in reviews or scholarly works.

Edited by Pam Lagomarsino, Above the Pages
Illustrations by Paul Joy, Hand Drawn Today
Back Cover Author photo by Jonathan Ho, Jonkelly Productions
Front Cover image by Frances Coch

ISBN: 978-1-7642759-0-3 paperback
978-1-7642759-1-0 eBook
First edition: September 2025
Printed in Australia by IngramSpark

None of the contents of this book has been created using artificial intelligence. All content and illustrations are the result of human creativity and collaboration.

Contents

Introduction	7
Chapter 1: Come to Me	9
Chapter 2: Follow Me	19
Chapter 3: Through Me	25
Chapter 4: Hear Me	29
Chapter 5: Believe in Me	34
Chapter 6: With the Father	39
Chapter 7: Remain in Me	46
Chapter 8: Marriage	64
Chapter 9: Holy Spirit	73
Chapter 10: Healing	85
Chapter 11: Deliverance	92
Chapter 12: Positioning Ourselves for Deliverance	103
Chapter 13: Freedom Prayers	119
Chapter 14: Prayer	134
Chapter 15: Praying for God's Will in Our Lives	147
Chapter 16: Prayers for Others	155
About the Author	163
About the Illustrator	164
Notes	165

Dedication

To my father, Maris, who taught me to pray, and to my mother, Jane, who willed me to write, thank you.

To my husband Phil, for endless conversations about faith during our many walks together. And to our three children, Emily, Liam, and Eva, your love has blessed me more than you can imagine.

Introduction

Have you ever tried to grow something wonderful? Maybe a tiny seed into a flourishing plant or nurturing an idea into a thriving business? If so, you understand just how essential it is to embrace and apply the principles of growth. With this knowledge, you can avoid the frustration of wasting time and resources and instead engage in accelerating your growth.

Nurturing a seed or an idea requires care and attentiveness to see it flourish, just as faith is something we cultivate by knowing the principles and putting them into practice.

As you progress in your faith journey as a new Christian, embracing the core principles of daily salvation, repentance, and forgiveness is essential for experiencing true freedom and breakthrough.

Prayer and Discipleship for New Christians provides the foundation for you to embrace your deliverance, freedom, and healing. It also instructs you on how to use Scripture to align your prayers with God's promises. Additionally, it offers practical guidance for living in Christ's righteousness.

Repetitive cycles of oppression can leave us feeling powerless and hopeless. But when we grasp the biblical principles that release spiritual growth and unlock God's abundant freedom, we can step into the freedom God's Word promises. This book offers you practical, Bible-based steps for you to grow and thrive.

It offers teaching and Scripture-based prayers, providing freedom steps for:

- healthy hearts,
- reconciled relationships and
- breakthrough from bondage.

After many years in ministry, I've noticed common themes people often bring up when seeking prayer. This insight inspired me to write down several prayers I've shared with those looking for freedom. While these aren't rigid scripts, they're meant to encourage you to apply Scripture confidently to your own prayers.

Use these prayers and declarations to show you how to use God's Scripture to pray in agreement with His best plans for you and your family. I pray your faith will grow strong and you and your family will flourish as you learn to trust God's goodness and power. In faith, it's time to pray bold prayers with the Holy Spirit and see your family live the freedom Jesus died for.

Chapter 1

Come to Me

I am the bread of life.

Have you ever noticed someone unfamiliar with you describe you in a way that doesn't truly capture who you are? Their impression fails to convey your character, skills, personality, or potential. You might have spoken up to correct their perception, or perhaps you just let it slide.

When God wanted to make Himself known to Moses, He called Himself 'I AM' (Exodus 3:14). These mysterious words referred to a timeless truth about God and His unchanging nature, concerning the past, present, and future of His eternal presence.

Jesus also chose to use the words 'I am' to convey His true identity. Many people were trying to understand, and He wanted to be clear about who He truly was and why He was here. Jesus made seven 'I am' statements that reveal both His identity and mission. The choice of seven 'I am' statements symbolise the completeness and perfection of His identity, as the biblical representation of the number seven denotes completion. All these statements are recorded in the gospel of John, where they accompany the many signs in the book. John tells us, 'But these are written so that you may believe that Jesus is the Messiah, the Son of God, and that by believing you may have life in his name' (John 20:31 CSB).

Paying attention to how Jesus describes Himself helps us understand His identity and why people choose to follow Him and make Him Lord of their lives.

In the gospel of John, we read about several signs that demonstrate Jesus is not only human but also divine. One of these signs was His prayer to multiply a child's portion of bread and fish. This miracle enabled Him to feed lunch to a crowd of thousands who had gathered to hear Him teach.

The next day, some of the crowd who had eaten the multiplied lunch searched for and found Him. Their belief in Him had been sparked by this miracle, not so much because they witnessed it, but more so because they experienced it with full stomachs after eating from the miracle.

When these people asked Jesus what God required of them, He explained they must believe in the One whom God had sent. They remembered the Israelites were able to believe when they received a sign from God, which was 'manna from heaven' in the wilderness. Manna was the ingredient to make fresh bread every day, which God allowed to fall from the sky each morning (Exodus 16). Considering that only the day before, God had prayed and multiplied one child's lunch to feed at least five thousand people, it's amazing they were asking for a sign (John 6:30) yet did not realise they had already received their sign, which was bread from heaven. But patiently, Jesus explained, 'I am the bread of life. Whoever comes to me will never go hungry, and whoever believes in me will never be thirsty' (John 6:35 NIV).

The purpose of Jesus' identity and ministry was always to become 'the Bread of Life.' Even His place of birth in Bethlehem was prophetically positioned. Bethlehem in Hebrew translates to 'the House of Bread.'[1]

Interestingly, Jesus clearly lays out who He is. He plainly states the two things He requires of those who wish to receive the Bread of Life: to come to Him and believe in Him. He was speaking to people who had spent the morning searching for Him, having chosen to seek Him out. They also asked what they needed to do now, and His response was to believe in Him. Yet some of those listening struggled to accept this message. They were considering Jesus as human while missing the fact He was also the Son of God and, therefore, divine in nature. They were confused and asked, 'Is this not Jesus, the son of Joseph whose father and mother we know? How can he say, "I came down from heaven"?' (John 6:42 NIV). It seems like a reasonable question, but this was asked just after the morning of His miracle of multiplying bread. This illustrates our belief must be stronger than our doubt.

Jesus explained how bread symbolises His body and wine symbolises His blood, and how the bread represents the forgiveness we receive from His death and resurrection. This forgiveness leads to eternal life, so He is the Bread of Life.

> Jesus said to them, "Very truly I tell you, unless you eat the flesh of the Son of Man and drink his blood, you have no life in you. Whoever eats my flesh and drinks my blood has eternal life, and I will raise them up at the last day. For my flesh is real food and my blood is real drink. Whoever eats my flesh and drinks my blood remains in me, and I in them. Just as the living Father sent me and I live because of the Father, so the one who feeds on me will live because of me. This is the bread that came down from heaven. Your ancestors ate manna and died, but whoever feeds on this bread will live forever."
>
> John 6:53–58 NIV

After Jesus revealed Himself as the Bread of Life, some listeners turned away and no longer followed Him. Lacking faith in Him, they chose not to believe. When we decide to come to Jesus, we must actively choose whether to follow Him. Jesus' true disciples not only came to Him but also made the choice to follow, finding satisfaction in the Bread of Life that would fulfil them for eternity. The personal decision to follow Him is expressed by our decision to make Jesus our Lord and Savior. This process is referred to as our salvation.

Salvation

Salvation is the act of being saved, rescued, or delivered from something dangerous or destructive. The power of our rescue flows through the relationship we share with the one who saves.

Relationship of Salvation

As Christians, we acknowledge we are saved by Jesus Christ, who, out of a relationship with us, offered His life for the forgiveness of our sins. We received this forgiveness while we were still sinners, making this act His grace to us. This grace is ongoing and is seen every time we receive God's undeserved favour. God's gift of grace is continually given to us through the love He shares in His relationship with us. Even though Jesus died only once, God continues to rescue us from sin and evil in the world, and we continue to receive His saving grace and the working of salvation in our lives.

We Can Choose Either a Relationship with God or a Relationship with Sin

If sin is left unforgiven, the consequences lead to separation from a relationship with God, both now and for eternity. Our forgiveness by Jesus and our relationship with God's Spirit grant us daily salvation from our attachment to sin.

Even for those who have decided to become Christians, Satan continues to tempt us, as it is his nature to seek, kill, and destroy. Therefore, it is up to us to determine which relationship holds more importance: our relationship with God or sin. It becomes a daily choice to live in God's salvation. Eventually, we come to understand that pursuing a relationship with God requires letting go of what grieves Him, which is sin. The sins we commit in moments of weakness and humanity are paid for, not by us, but by Jesus. Our debt is wiped clean on our behalf. Similarly, if we continue to pursue a relationship with sin, this will also carry a cost, which results in a life and eternity marked by separation from God.

What About Sacrifice?

Motivated by His love and relationship with us, God gave His Son, Jesus, as a sacrifice so that our penalty for sin could be cancelled completely. In preparation for this, God prepared Jesus for what would happen and worked with Jesus' willingness to die. Like the lambs that had been sacrificed before, Jesus attempted to atone for sin; however, Jesus' death fulfilled the ultimate sacrifice. Consequently, sacrifices would no longer be necessary, and Jesus became known as the slain Lamb.

Everyone Is Invited

Even the earliest humans—Adam and Eve—who experienced daily closeness with God, also required salvation from sin. After being tempted by Satan and committing their sin, they faced the dire consequences of both physical and spiritual separation from God. This must have been incredibly lonely after having such a close relationship with Him. Paul pointed out that we, too, have sinned, 'For all have sinned and fall short of the glory of God' (Romans 3:23 NIV). It's understandable that Adam and Eve sinned, being human, as we all have encountered temptation and sinned. Consequently, we have all experienced that overwhelming sensation of shame and guilt.

Adam and Eve, the first humans to sin, tried to make amends with God through sacrifices and offerings. Yet, these efforts failed to restore the closeness and intimacy intended in the daily relationship between God and humanity.

Four thousand years after Adam and Eve left Eden and their close relationship with God, He sent His Son Jesus to deal with this separation once and for all. Upon Jesus' death, the veil that separated humanity from a personal connection with God was torn. This extraordinary event allowed everyone the opportunity to join God's family and restore a close relationship with Him. The invitation is extended to all, irrespective of race, gender, financial circumstances, or social standing. God has no favourites; His love is complete and unique for each person.

It is natural to feel uncertain about navigating feelings of sin, shame, and guilt. No matter how hard we try, our best efforts alone can't truly remove those burdens, and striving for goodness doesn't bring us any closer to God. Fortunately, Christianity offers an amazing solution: through Jesus, we are forgiven, and our shame is wiped away. This grace is what truly restores our connection with God, bridging the gap we might feel.

How to Accept the Invitation

Accepting this invitation to draw closer to God through the forgiveness of our sins occurs by having faith in Jesus Christ. This faith—believing He lived, died, and rose again, conquering sin, death, and illness through His shed blood for our freedom, along with the resurrection power of the Holy Spirit—brings new hope and life to those who wish to be reborn in Christ.

Jesus's rescue act allows us to live in the daily grace that results from allowing God to be our one true God. Accepting that Jesus personally died for our sins to be forgiven enables Him to be our Shepherd, guiding us by His Spirit, who provides wisdom and direction.

Below, I provide a step-by-step explanation of how the decision for personal salvation works. Additionally, I've included a prayer for salvation. If you have not yet invited Jesus to be your personal Lord and Saviour, I invite you to pray the prayer below and to sincerely believe Jesus loves you. He lived, died, and rose again so that you could be forgiven and overcome sin and evil. You can discover your identity as God's child and maintain a relationship with Him today, tomorrow, and for eternity.

How Salvation Occurs

1. We are drawn to Jesus by the power of His Holy Spirit. 'No one can come to me unless the Father who sent me draws them, and I will raise them up at the last day,' (John 6:44 ESV). God sends the Holy Spirit to reach our hearts and lead us to God through Jesus. The way the Holy Spirit draws individuals to Jesus is unique. Because the Holy Spirit knows our hearts so intimately, He makes us aware of Him. This can happen through His involvement in our circumstances or through dreams, visions, or prompting conversations with other Christians. It may also be by the Holy Spirit connecting with us during our hardships. These are just a few examples of how the Holy Spirit reaches out to individuals to draw them to Jesus.

2. We believe and confess Jesus is Lord, that He died and was raised from the dead. 'If you declare with your mouth, "Jesus is Lord," and believe in your heart that God raised him from the dead, you will be saved' (Romans 10:9 NIV). There is a moment when we exercise our free will to choose Jesus and to choose God. We decide we are willing to be led by God and saved by Christ's death and resurrection.

3. We are sealed by God with the Holy Spirit. This is akin to our adoption ceremony, marking our entry into a covenant relationship with God as our Father and affirming our position as His child. 'And you also were included in Christ when you heard the message of truth, the gospel of your salvation. When you believed, you were marked in him with a seal, the promised Holy Spirit' (Ephesians 1:13 NIV). I like to envision this as a holy moment where God anoints our forehead with oil, placing His seal of the Holy Spirit.

Personal Prayer of Salvation

God, I thank You for Your Holy Spirit, which has opened my eyes to Your love. Your kindness and patience lead me to repentance, allowing me to say I am sorry for my sins, and I need You. I'm sorry for living independently from You. For following the easy path that leads to destruction, please forgive me. I acknowledge Your Son, Jesus Christ, died on the cross for the forgiveness of my sins, and on the third day, He rose again by the power of the Holy Spirit. I receive your forgiveness and accept your love in my heart, mind, body, and memories.

I accept Your Son, Jesus Christ, as my Lord and Saviour to follow Him all the days of my life. I ask You, Father God, to adopt me as Your child. I choose to live with You and follow You as Your disciple from this day forward. Please grant Your Holy Spirit to guide me in Your wisdom and love.

I choose to travel on a new road that leads to true life. As I read the Bible, may Your words guide me in finding the way to walk and live, revealing Your desire for my life. I pray You would help me find Christian friends to learn alongside and help me grow in my faith. I thank You, Father God, for the greatest gift You could ever give me: everlasting life with You. In Jesus' name, Amen.

If you have just said this prayer for the first time, I encourage you to tell somebody else who has made the commitment to become a follower of Christ. Write down the date as it is a date for you to celebrate forevermore.

Chapter 2

Follow Me

I am the light of the world.

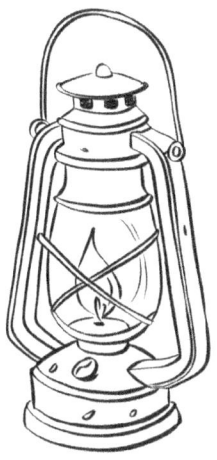

Many people are afraid of the dark because of what might be lurking within it. The unknown can feel threatening. It's amazing how even the tiniest crack of light from beneath a closed door or the smallest sliver of moonlight can illuminate the stark darkness, helping us feel less lost and afraid. You have probably noticed that when the power goes out, the first thing you reach for is some source of light.

Interestingly, twice, Jesus referred to Himself as 'the light of the world' (John 8:12, 9:5). His light was a light that would reveal what is hidden in darkness and shine clearly on the truth.

Following one of His references, He demonstrated the power of His light by physically bringing light to a vulnerable man whom He had passed by every day. He did this by miraculously healing his eyes from lifelong blindness, as the man had been blind since birth (John 9:1–7). People had become so used to this man that they likely walked past him several times a day, year after year. By Jesus enabling this man, who could neither work nor live a functional life, He revealed Himself as the source of light in his darkness.

Jesus' messages conveyed He was not only the light for our physical blindness but also a beacon against spiritual darkness. More broadly, He demonstrated Himself as the source of light in our personal darkness, including the hidden areas of captivity, as well as the darkness in the world. Jesus' mission was to bring light into the world, revealing the hidden lies, doubts, confusion, and misconceptions that leave humanity lost and grasping for truth.

However, to receive this light, He requires us to do one thing: follow Him to stay close to the light source. For those who choose to follow Him, Jesus promises to be a light source so that we can see the truth and the way to freedom. When Jesus spoke again to the people, He said, 'I am the light of the world. Whoever follows me will never walk in darkness but will have the light of life' (John 8:12 ESV). This aspect of Jesus is vital for us, as we all share the same need for light. Each of us faces times of challenge and uncertainty when we are lost, if not for the light of Jesus. In Psalm 23:4, David shares this insight about Jesus: 'Even though I walk through the darkest valley, I will fear no evil, for you are with me' (NIV).

We find our way out of darkness into freedom from the light Jesus shines.

Jesus takes this analogy even further when He tells His followers they are also a light to the world. By receiving His light, it becomes alive in us to display His glory for the world to see. Jesus says, 'You are the light of the world. A town built on a hill cannot be hidden. Neither do people light a lamp and put it under a bowl. Instead, they put it on its stand, and it gives light to everyone in the house. In the same way, let your light shine before others, that they may see your good deeds and glorify your Father in heaven' (Matthew 5:14–16 NIV). Collectively, as followers of Christ, the church shines the light of Jesus, illuminating truth and light to their homes, cities, country, and ultimately the world.

As we gravitate to the light of Jesus and allow it to illuminate through us, it is important we acknowledge sin in our lives. Because of the grace we receive from Jesus, we can be honest with God about the sins we need to surrender and turn away from. His response is not to shame us, but instead to bring us out of any areas of darkness and allow us to live freely in His light.

The Power of Repentance

If you had to guess the topic of Jesus' very first message, what would you say? Well, Jesus's first lesson was about the importance of repentance! 'From that time Jesus began to preach, saying Repent: for the kingdom of heaven is at hand' (Matthew 4:17 KJV). If this is the first message Jesus wanted His disciples to learn, then it should have our full attention. To enjoy the freedom we find in Jesus and make the kingdom of God accessible to us now, we need to resist Satan and turn away from sin. Living out of our reverence for God in this way creates a platform for wisdom to flow through us.

I remember stopping at a petrol station to fill up my car. When I got out of the car, I saw a man yelling at a young woman because he had bumped her car with his. Yes, he bumped into her, but he was the one yelling instead of providing her with the information that she was asking him for. Despite his error, he was telling her the small dent in her car didn't matter, and she shouldn't worry about it. The girl was silent and visibly shocked. When I walked past, I asked what was going on. When he looked up at me, I said, 'She is only doing what her father has likely taught her to do after an accident.' At this, the girl nodded in agreement. To my surprise, the man immediately started to cry. He told the girl he was sorry, and the car wasn't his; he had borrowed it from his friend. His demeanour drastically changed the situation for the young woman he had bumped into. He apologised and eventually stopped making excuses. His humility made it possible for the young woman to sort out the arrangements with him so that they could both get on with their day.

In the same way, we need to approach God with humility regarding our mistakes and regrets. God wants us to show remorse when we turn from Him or harm His people. The practice of approaching God with a repentant heart is particularly significant for our prayer life. Our confession during prayer is what creates a posture of humility towards God. Paul describes it this way: 'Repent, then, and turn to God, so that your sins may be wiped out, that times of refreshing may come from the Lord' (Acts 3:19 NIV). The spiritual act of humbling ourselves to apologise to God and express our regret for our mistakes opens a spiritual and physical avenue for God to refresh and renew our hearts and bodies. It helps us live in a genuine and authentic relationship, inviting Him into our struggles and seeking His strength for our weaknesses.

A Prayer of Repentance

I open my heart in truth before You, Lord, and allow You to wash me of my sins and mistakes—the things I have done and said that have hurt others and myself. Please forgive me, Lord, for (Share them with Him now from your heart).

I release these to You now, Lord. I lay them down at the foot of the cross to never pick them up again. I accept that the blood of Jesus purifies me. Jesus is interceding for me, and based on my confession, I embrace the pardon, forgiveness, and grace that Jesus laid down His life to give me. I receive that unconditional grace from You, my Father in heaven. The vastness of Your forgiveness for me is as far as the east is from the west, and You think of my sin no more.

I accept the everlasting life You have lavishly given me to live every day. Thank You, Father God; thank You, Jesus. Spirit of God, please lead me in all truth and righteousness. I need You to guide me in Your holiness so that I may resist evil and walk in righteousness and obedience to Your Word.

Chapter 3

Through Me

I am the Door of the Sheep.

It's interesting to consider that at one point, several great Jewish patriarchs or prophets worked as shepherds. These included Abraham, Isaac, Jacob, Joseph, David, and Amos. While they all physically cared for their sheep, God also used them as leaders of people.

Many generations later, as Jesus ministered, he engaged in a pivotal conversation with the Pharisees, who were the religious leaders of the time. These Pharisees had just shown cruelty to the blind man whom Jesus had healed. Jesus used this conversation about sheep and shepherds to contrast their cruel hearts as leaders with His leadership mission of caring for his people and guiding them to God.

He specifically highlighted the image of a 'door' (some Bible translations use the word 'gate') and referred to the door as the entry point for His sheep to be saved and find freedom. This symbol of a door perfectly revealed His purpose as the entry point for people not only to enter but also to be saved in finding God.

> Therefore, Jesus said again, 'Very truly I tell you, I am the gate for the sheep. All who have come before me are thieves and robbers, but the sheep have not listened to them. I am the gate; whoever enters through me will be saved. They will come in and go out, and find pasture. The thief comes only to steal and kill and destroy; I have come that they may have life, and have it to the full.'
>
> John 10:7–10 NIV

Jesus warned of the dangers posed by spiritual leaders who bypass the gate. Only through the gate, Jesus, can we find safe pasture and be saved. He revealed the Pharisees and many like them were false shepherds, intending to harm the sheep, just as they were cruel to the blind man who Jesus healed. By jumping over the fence, the Pharisees bypassed the true path to freedom, which is through Jesus. 'Jesus answered, "I am the way and the truth and the life. No one comes to the Father except through me"' (John 14:6 NIV).

As Christians today, we choose to walk through the door of Jesus, finding God not only as our Saviour but also newly positioned to enjoy the green pastures of freedom through Him. Our public profession of faith and choice to reach God through the door of Jesus is publicly demonstrated through our baptism.

Water Baptism

The first example of baptism in the New Testament comes from Jesus' cousin, John the Baptist, who shared a powerful message of repentance. The people John preached to were encouraged to prepare their hearts for the Messiah. For those who participated in their baptism of repentance, their washing in the waters of the River Jordan provided an opportunity to confess their sins, acknowledge their need for purification, and express their readiness for the Messiah, whom they would ultimately find in Jesus.

Just before Jesus began His public ministry, He was baptised by John the Baptist in the Jordan River. Jesus' baptism demonstrated His obedience to the Father, His Father's public endorsement of Jesus as His Son, and His receiving of the Holy Spirit. These events were pivotal in launching Jesus' public ministry.

After Jesus' death and resurrection, the baptisms continued. Many of these baptisms were prompted as a response to the preaching of the apostle Philip, whose words were empowered by the Holy Spirit. Samaritans who had not been freely accepted by Judean Jews prior to this point were included in the invitation to become baptised. This was revolutionary for the customs and culture. 'But when they believed Philip as he preached the things concerning the kingdom of God and the name of Jesus Christ, both men and women were baptized' (Acts 8:12 NKJV). The importance of participating in Christ's death and resurrection was an important part of their public statement of faith in Christ Jesus.

This inclusion of baptism for the Samaritans extends to us today. Water baptism is a baptism into Christ. It signifies our death to old, sinful ways and being born again with Christ. As we go under the water, we share in Christ's death. Just as Jesus was raised to life after His death, in our baptism we are also raised to new life as we emerge from the waters. The biblical example of baptism in water serves as a symbolic public declaration of our faith in Christ and our alignment with His death and resurrection.

Chapter 4

Hear Me

I am the Good Shepherd.

The role of a shepherd is to call and lead their sheep, as well as to protect and save them from danger. In the Old Testament, we can read of David, who wrestled both a bear and a lion to save his flock. In doing so, he demonstrated the protective nature of a shepherd to the point of risking his own life for the flock.

Around one thousand years later, Jesus' willingness to lay down His life for us, His sheep, demonstrates His deep, abiding commitment to us as His people, the sheep of His pasture, and also reveals His profound obedience to God.

I am the good shepherd. The good shepherd lays down his life for the sheep. The hired hand is not the shepherd and does not own the sheep. So when he sees the wolf coming, he abandons the sheep and runs away. Then the wolf attacks the flock and scatters it. The man runs away because he is a hired hand and cares nothing for the sheep.

I am the good shepherd; I know my sheep and my sheep know me—just as the Father knows me and I know the Father—and I lay down my life for the sheep. I have other sheep that are not of this sheep pen. I must bring them also. They too will listen to my voice, and there shall be one flock and one shepherd. The reason my Father loves me is that I lay down my life—only to take it up again. No one takes it from me, but I lay it down of my own accord. I have authority to lay it down and authority to take it up again. This command I received from my Father.

John 10:11–18 NIV

Jesus refers to including sheep who are not from His flock, meaning those who were not born Jewish. In fact, the sheep who hear His voice can follow Him, regardless of which flock they started in. This invitation is open to all who wish to follow the voice of the Shepherd who would lay down His life for them.

I live in Australia, a country known for its many sheep. I love learning about the different sounds sheep herders use to identify themselves to their sheep. Each sound is so unique and distinctive that the sheep do not hesitate to follow. We who choose to follow

Jesus must tune into His voice, which we discover as we read the Bible. His words guide us, protect us, and lead us to God.

One way Jesus protects us from danger is by our willingness to follow His commands. He is a Shepherd who wants to protect us from evil and trouble. We call this obedience to His authority, 'the fear of the Lord,' which has a deeper meaning than we initially realise. Just as Jesus was willing to lay down His life for the sheep, we need to be willing to lay down our lives to live with Christ; we can do this by living in obedience to Him.

Fear of the Lord

The fear of the Lord is a topic that intrigues Christians, as it goes deeper than our initial thoughts when we hear the phrase 'fear of the Lord.' I have had several conversations with people genuinely seeking to understand this subject and its relationship to Christianity. The question that often arises is, 'When we are taught so strongly that God is a God of love, how can we possibly be asked to consider the fear of the Lord?' Let's recognise there are four different types of fear:

1. practical fear,
2. tormenting/demonic fear,
3. fear of man, and
4. fear of God.

Practical fear prevents us from burning our hands on the stove or falling off the edge of a cliff. It differs from demonic fear, which is assigned to torment us. Fear of man keeps us confined and undermines our ability to live confidently. The fear of the Lord is not negative; rather, it enables us to draw from the abundance of His Holy Spirit.

Obedience to His Word brings a significant harvest into our lives. God doesn't want us to be scared of Him, but He requires us to live with such reverence for His power that we desire to do and say what is holy and to detest what is sinful. It involves esteeming God higher than anyone or anything else, including ourselves. Our love for God guards us against legalism, while our fear of God protects us from lawlessness and recklessness.

What Flows out from the Fear of the Lord?

- **Life** - 'Fear of the LORD leads to life, bringing security and protection from harm.' (Proverbs 19:23 NLT)

- **Knowledge** - 'The fear of the Lord is the beginning of knowledge; but fools despise wisdom and instruction.' (Proverbs 1:7 KJV)

- **Wisdom** - 'The fear of the LORD is the beginning of wisdom, and knowledge of the Holy One is understanding.' (Proverbs 9:10 NIV)

- **Understanding** - 'And unto man he said, Behold, the fear of the Lord, that is wisdom; and to depart from evil is understanding.' (Job 28:28 KJV)

When we consider the sun, we recognise its power and necessity. We understand that if it were even a tiny bit closer, we would all burn to death. Similarly, if it were tilted slightly further away, we would easily freeze to death. We appreciate the beauty and warmth of the sun, which we seek to bask in. In the same way, we acknowledge

God's all-consuming power, and in this awareness, we desire to bask in the goodness of His warmth and intimacy. Living in the blessing of the fear of the Lord allows us to flow in security and protection in our lives. It provides us with the knowledge we need to operate in His wisdom, knowledge, and understanding. As people of prayer, we require knowledge, wisdom, and understanding to pray in alignment with both God's heart and the genuine needs around us.

Chapter 5

Believe in Me

I Am the Resurrection and the Life.

By far, my absolute favourite miracle of Jesus is when He prayed for His deceased friend Lazarus. The way Jesus approached this was filled with love and compassion, which deeply grips my heart.

Jesus didn't hide His love for Lazarus; in fact, His love was obvious to others. While Lazarus was still alive, one of Lazarus' sisters, Martha, came to Jesus and said, 'Lord, the one you love is sick' (John 11:3 ESV). This is the love He shares with each of us—an obvious love for us to receive.

Even though Jesus loved Lazarus, He waited to go to him, allowing the upcoming miracle to help people believe in His power as the One who brings resurrection and life. After being informed that Lazarus had died, 'Jesus told them plainly, "Lazarus is dead, and for your sake I am glad I was not there, so that you may believe. But let us go to him"' (John 11:14–15 ESV). The words may sound confronting, and we could misunderstand His intentions, but we need to remember He spoke with full knowledge of what He was on His way to do. Jesus was speaking out of love for the miracle witnesses, to help them believe.

By the time Jesus arrived, Lazarus had been dead in the tomb for four days! When Martha questioned Jesus for taking so long, He replied, 'I am the resurrection and the life. The one who believes in me will live, even though they die; and whoever lives by believing in me will never die. Do you believe this?' (John 11:25–26 NIV). Her reply showed great faith, as it was before the miracle had actually occurred: '"Yes, Lord," she replied, "I believe that you are the Messiah, the Son of God, who is to come into the world"' (John 11:27 NIV). Jesus' power to defeat death is essential within the Christian faith. With Jesus as the resurrection and the life, both sin and death are overcome, enabling both His and our resurrection and eternal life.

When Lazarus' other sister, Mary, came to Jesus, crying and brokenhearted, Jesus' heart was moved with compassion. 'When Jesus saw her weeping, and the Jews who had come along with her also weeping, he was deeply moved in spirit and troubled. "Where have you laid him?" he asked. "Come and see, Lord," they replied. Jesus wept. Then the Jews said, "See how he loved him!"' (John 11:33–36 NIV). Jesus was not troubled because He was worried about Lazarus; instead, He was troubled because of the reality of human suffering. Because His heart empathised with Mary, we must remember that in all our tribulations, Jesus cares, yet in all this empathy, He is the resurrection and the life.

When they reached the tomb, it had a strong smell of death.

Then Jesus said, "Did I not tell you that if you believe, you will see the glory of God?" So they took away the stone. Then Jesus looked up and said, "Father, I thank You that You have heard me. I knew You always hear me, but I said this for the benefit of the people standing here, that they may believe that you sent me." When he had said this, Jesus called in a loud voice, "Lazarus, come out!" The dead man came out, his hands and feet wrapped with strips of linen, and a cloth around his face. Jesus said to them, "Take off the grave clothes and let him go" (John 11:40-44 NIV).

Our belief in Jesus' power to bring resurrection and life was so significant that He was willing to allow built-up tension to demonstrate it. We must be ready to believe Jesus is the resurrection and life, even during our most intense struggles.

One way we stir our belief in receiving His resurrection and life is by partaking of His power during Communion.

Communion/Eucharist

The evening before Jesus's crucifixion, He joyfully celebrated the Passover festival, a time when the firstborn Jewish males were spared from death by God's grace. During this meaningful dinner, Jesus shared profound teachings about the significance of His blood and broken body. This message held a surprising depth, especially given the events that were about to unfold, leaving the disciples in a state of wonder as they sought to comprehend it. This special gathering is now known as The Last Supper, or Maundy Thursday, as we approach the celebration of Easter.

Jesus wanted to prepare His disciples with an understanding of the power that forgiveness would bring. 'While they were eating, Jesus took bread, and when he had given thanks, he broke it and gave it to his disciples, saying, "Take and eat; this is my body." Then he took a cup, and when he had given thanks, he gave it to them, saying, "Drink from it, all of you. This is my blood of the new covenant, which is poured out for many for the forgiveness of sins"' (Matthew 26:26–28 NIV).

The practice of Communion serves as a reminder of the new promise we have with Jesus. For this reason, churches practice this with symbols. Offering wine or juice to church attendees symbolises His blood, with crackers or bread representing His broken body, given for the forgiveness of our sins. Partaking of Communion is a powerful way to engage with the forgiveness, healing, and redemption of Christ. This can be done in church, at home with family, in a Bible study, in a fellowship group, or with your spouse. It is a significant act within marriages that reinstates the deep connection with Christ and with your spouse. Relationally, this practice can help restore unity during times of struggle, particularly as you confess your mistakes to each other during Communion. A house divided cannot stand, but couples and families who humble themselves before God and each other will establish a strong spiritual unity that Satan cannot penetrate.

It's intriguing that when Jesus' disciples heard His teachings about the significance of His broken body and shed blood, they were unaware that His death was imminent. They could not fully comprehend the reasons behind His explanation of the symbols signifying the forgiveness of their sins through His blood and broken body. Despite spending the last three and a half years with Him, they often struggled to grasp His messages until they witnessed the realisation of them. Many of His miracles began with teaching, followed by healing or a miracle. So this was the teaching before His miracle of death and resurrection. They would see the risen Lord, leading to a complete understanding of the fulfilment of Jesus' mission to redeem the world.

As disciples, we often find ourselves unsure about what lies ahead—what new teachings Jesus will share with us, what healings or miracles we will experience. Yet, one thing we hold on to is the certainty that Jesus' words are preparing our hearts for the unknown tomorrow. We can trust the power of His broken body and blood is more than enough for whatever tomorrow may bring. We can step into tomorrow with confidence because we are embraced by the promise of His sacrifice. Through His death and resurrection, He has gifted us the strength to overcome, heal, and receive His miracles in our lives.

Chapter 6

With the Father

I Am the Way, the Truth, and the Life.

During my time in pastoral ministry, I've often been struck by the shift in conversation in people nearing the end of their lives. As they prepare to leave this world, many speak from a different perspective—one that seems to cut through life's distractions and offer a rare clarity and encouragement to those they love. Their words often carry a weighty importance, which at times has lingered in my mind and prompted me to reflect more deeply on their meaning. It seems that for many people, the emotional and spiritual transition from this life to the next brings about a shift in priorities, thinking, and perspective.

Jesus explained to the disciples where He would be going, describing the rooms in heaven which He would prepare for them. This message was preparing them for His departure, but it was also revealing His intention to return. Although they did not understand what He was referring to, they asked Him to show them the way because they wanted to follow Him. 'Jesus answered, "I am the way and the truth and the life. No one comes to the Father except through me"' (John 14:6 NIV).

At first glance, Jesus' statement here may remind us of His earlier declaration: "I am the gate." But when we look more closely, we see He includes something significant: "the way, the truth, and the life." These words aren't just poetic—they provide depth to our understanding of how we find God through Jesus. They show us coming to the Father involves a journey (the way), an unveiling of divine reality (the truth), and the gift of eternal relationship (the life).

Belief enables us to follow Jesus on this path. To hear His voice of truth and receive the life He offers, we must be willing to believe. Even faith as small as a mustard seed is enough—but we must be willing to live in the truth of who Jesus is: one with the Father.

Jesus goes on to say: 'Anyone who has seen me has seen the Father. How can you say, "Show us the Father"? Don't you believe that I am in the Father, and that the Father is in me? The words I say to you I do not speak on my own authority. Rather, it is the Father, living in me, who is doing his work. Believe me when I say that I am in the Father and the Father is in me' (John 14:9–11 NIV).

Here, it's important to realise Jesus chooses to remain in God, and God chooses to remain in Jesus. They are so connected that although they are separate, they are also one. Jesus' words in this moment reveal a deeper level of His relationship with God, and they offer insight to those seeking to follow Him. In Jesus' words, we find a glimpse into the divine intimacy He shares with the Father. And then, remarkably, He invites us into that relationship through belief in Him.

'Very truly I tell you, whoever believes in me will do the works I have been doing, and they will do even greater things than these, because I am going to the Father. And I will do whatever you ask in my name, so that the Father may be glorified in the Son. You may ask me for anything in my name, and I will do it' (John 14:12–14 NIV).

Jesus empowers us not only to believe but to participate in the work of God—living in faith, asking in His name, and glorifying the Father through our lives. It is a powerful and humbling invitation into a divine partnership, made possible by the One who is the way, the truth, and the life.

As we journey with Jesus, we do so from a sincere heart. We must use wisdom to guard our hearts from the dangers of bitterness, which inevitably robs us of flowing effectively in love.

Healthy Hearts

Taking care of our hearts through healthy checks can become a daily routine for our spiritual well-being. King Solomon wisely advised us that 'Above all else, guard your heart, for everything you do flows from it'(Proverbs 4:23 ESV). For children, this wonderful habit can be lovingly passed down by parents or caring adults who recognise the importance of guiding them in foundational Christian practices. When learned from a young age, these daily spiritual practices can support us throughout our lives. 'Train up a child in the way he should go: and when he is old, he will not depart from it' (Proverbs 22:6 KJV).

Peter, one of Jesus' disciples, asked Jesus about the limits of forgiveness.

> Then Peter came to Jesus and asked, "Lord, how many times shall I forgive my brother or sister who sins against me? Up to seven times?" Jesus answered, "I tell you, not seven times, but seventy-seven times." (Matthew 18:21-22 NIV).

Jesus emphasises the importance of continuously forgiving, demonstrating His concern for our emotional well-being. A light and healthy heart stems from our readiness to forgive those whose words, actions, and behaviours have caused hurt, pain, and even trauma in our lives.

Jesus clearly emphasises the crucial importance of forgiveness in our relationships with God and others. He states, 'For if you forgive other people when they sin against you, your heavenly father will also forgive you. But if you do not forgive others their sins, your father will not forgive your sins' (Matthew 6:14–15 NIV). The essence of forgiveness lies in maintaining a pure heart before God. We relinquish the resentment and the desire for revenge that those who hurt us may deserve. By choosing to forgive, we invite God's peace to envelop our hearts, allowing us to move forward lightly and pray from a position of peace and purity.

It's important to note forgiveness is not about deciding offences caused aren't so bad after all; it's also not about deciding our feelings don't really matter and we should instead suppress our emotions. Instead, we must honestly acknowledge the sin of others for what it truly is and take the weight of it off our hearts by forgiving the person behind the sin. We should freely apply God's grace to the person through our own will and decision as an act of obedience to God.

Often, our emotions lead us into sin. As an extreme example, murder often begins with the emotions of anger and hatred. For the person who hasn't learned to rule over their emotions, the consequences are tragic. We need to acknowledge our emotions and allow them to be explored and understood. Yet the person who cannot rule their emotions will be easily led into sin. When Jesus instructed us not to sin in our anger, He didn't say not to experience anger. Our weapon to rule over anger is to praise God for who He is and what He has done—to turn our hearts towards God and thank Him for His immense grace. When we can rule over our emotions, we can be trusted to steward and grow people. When we can forgive others' sins towards us, we can live in the peace of not being reliant on other people to give us peace. We can grow in maturity and live in the peace and joy God intended for us.

It's natural to still feel hurt and pain even after practising forgiveness; this reaction is to be expected. Practising forgiveness aligns us with Christ's teachings and His example. Eventually, our emotions will need to align with our decisions. The apostle Paul advises us to 'bear with each other and forgive one another if any of you has a grievance against someone. Forgive as the Lord forgave you. And over all these virtues put on love, which binds them all together in perfect unity' (Colossians 3:13–14 NIV). Our love for God and Jesus, along with our commitment to His teachings, forms a solid foundation for forgiving others. As we grow in love, we can learn to love those who have hurt us.

Steps to Healthy Heart Checks for Adults

1. **Reflect**

Are any events or conversations weighing on my heart, ruminating in my mind? (allow space to reflect).

2. **Write or consider**

Either write or think about what happened, what was said, and how it made me feel.

3. **Allow**

Allow myself to be honest about how it made me feel without diminishing the emotional effects that I have experienced.

4. **Release**

Tell God what happened (even though He already knows). Give the situation to Him. Invite Him into the situation. Tell God that even in my hurt, I choose to forgive and release the situation to Him.

An example of a forgiveness prayer might sound like:

I choose to forgive (name) for taking credit for my idea. This is the third time this has happened, and when my boss praised his idea, I felt unheard and frustrated, and I wanted to leave my work team. However, God, despite these feelings, I decide to follow Your guidance. So, I'm choosing to forgive (name) for claiming my idea as his own. Lord, I invite You into this part of my life and into future meetings with my team. Please grant me deep wisdom from Your Holy Spirit and fill my heart with peace, God. I love You, thank You for helping me let this go. In Jesus' name, Amen.

Tip: Don't excuse or justify the offence. Allow your feelings to be validated and then release the burden on your heart.

Steps to Healthy Heart Checks for Children

Parents/adults to guide children through the following steps:

1. **Ask:**

Is there anything making your heart unsettled, sad, or mad today? (allow space for them to reflect).

2. **Allow:**

Allow your child to share their concern about the incident or event that they have highlighted.

3. **Prompt**

Ask your child to explore if their heart may have been hurt or offended during the incident or event.

4. **Guide**

Guide your child in expressing forgiveness towards the person or people.

Example of guided support. This might sound like:

I choose to forgive (name) for calling me short today. It made me feel like I wasn't important. I forgive him for being unkind with his words. Please wash peace over my heart, God. I love You. Thank You for helping me let that go. In Jesus' name, Amen.

Tip: Don't excuse or justify the offence. Allow their feelings to be validated and then release the burden on their heart.

Chapter 7

Remain in Me

I Am the True Vine.

I am the vine; you are the branches.
If you remain in me and I in you, you will bear
much fruit; apart from me you can do nothing.

John 15:5 NIV

Last year, I planted three citrus trees: lime, lemon, and orange. All three have been watered daily, so I was curious why the orange tree was so much smaller and slightly shrivelled. I posted a photo in a gardening forum seeking advice. The feedback people offered me was surprising. They noticed from a shadow in the photo that the lime and lemon had full light all morning and day, while the orange tree, due to its planting position, had morning shade. It's incredible how much bigger and stronger the lime and lemon trees are because of their position in full sun.

Jesus, who said, 'I am the light of the world,' is the full sun we need to bear fruit. Remaining in Him allows us to grow the fruit that comes from His Spirit, just as Jesus remains in God and God remains in Jesus. We are invited to remain in Jesus and let Him remain in us. By doing this, Jesus promises to produce fruit in our lives.

Sometimes, God allows us to experience pruning so that He can cut away the dead wood in our lives. Like any good vine keeper, it is for our health that He allows us to be reshaped into His likeness and discard the heavy, dead branches that hinder us from producing healthy, good fruit.

Paul lists the fruit of the Holy Spirit as being 'love, joy, peace, forbearance, kindness, goodness, faithfulness, gentleness and self-control' (Galatians 5:22–23 NIV). Christians producing flourishing families, relationships, and ministries are also referred to as fruitful because of Christ working in their lives as they remain in Jesus.

Remaining in Jesus also enables us to live in His holiness, which is often called the righteousness of Christ.

Living in Christ's Righteousness

Paul's letter to the church in Ephesus offers valuable insights into how we should strive to live in accordance with God's righteousness. In Ephesians 4:1–5, Paul encourages Christians to walk in a manner worthy of their calling. While each of us has a unique calling within the body of Christ, Paul emphasises a common set of qualities we should aspire to embody through God's grace. These are:

Humility

Humility is the first virtue Paul mentions in this section of Ephesians. This is for good reason, as humility is the foundation upon which each additional virtue is built. Humility is so essential in our relationships that God's response is to provide a reward. Many verses speak of the value of humility, highlighting how precious it is to God and the powerful way He can work through those who embody it. This is why Scripture says: 'God opposes the proud but shows favour to the humble' (James 4:6 NIVUK). Those who live with humility are granted the reward and blessing of walking in the favour of God!

Humility truly transforms our relationships! Our hearts, attitudes, and interactions with others are influenced by either our humility or our ego. The interesting thing about humility is its connection to our security and identity in God. Those without a complete identity often struggle with an insecurity labelled as 'ego.' Living out of our security in God, which expresses itself as humility, brings with it an added promise: 'Humble yourselves before the Lord, and he will exalt you' (James 4:10 ESV). 'For whoever exalts himself will be humbled, and whoever humbles himself will be exalted' (Matthew 23:12 VOICE). God aims to uplift Christians who embody humility, as the Holy Spirit can work through them with ease and effectiveness. He seeks leaders and influencers who can be humble, as humility creates openness for the Holy Spirit to operate within us.

Humility is essential for prayer. Jesus taught that Christians should pray from a hidden place, reflecting a state of humility. 'When you pray, you should go into your room and close the door and pray to your Father who cannot be seen. Your Father can see what is done in secret, and he will reward you' (Matthew 6:6 NCV). Jesus illustrates the link between prayer and humility, emphasising that we pray from our relationship with God, dedicating quality time to Him in private rather than seeking recognition from others. In this humble setting, our hearts align with God's heart and His provision. According to Jesus, praying from this secret place also comes with rewards—these rewards may look different at various times. For example, there are the responses to our prayers, and at times, God's activity in paving the way for us without us even being aware of it. Regardless of the reward, it is given in response to our humility.

Gentleness

Gentleness is one fruit of the Holy Spirit. The seeds of gentleness produce growth, trust, and flourishing relationships. Those who walk in gentleness are well-positioned to nurture others. This applies to raising children, in the workplace, and to Christian discipleship.

The apostle Paul emphasises the importance of a gentle spirit in his advice to fathers. However, it applies to all parents: 'Fathers, do not provoke your children to anger, but bring them up in the discipline and instruction of the Lord' (Ephesians 6:4 ESV). It is this gentle approach that enables parents to discipline within a relationship. It's ineffective to discipline a child based on a higher level of relationship that we share with them. Therefore, gentleness builds the trust we need to influence children's lives and guide them into maturity.

Gentleness fosters the growth of others and is especially important in nurturing their faith. A kind word sows seeds that will flourish. This principle extends across all sectors, including the church, business, medicine, and education; gentle individuals earn trust, enabling them to convey truth and enhance the learning process. Families, churches, and workplaces benefit greatly from leaders who embody a gentle spirit.

Patience

One of the bravest prayers you can ever pray is 'Lord, teach me patience.' The answer to this prayer is likely to lead to some tests! We all know patience is very hard to produce from our natural selves, because patience is a fruit of the Holy Spirit and flows out of a life lived together with the Holy Spirit.

Patience in itself is the will to wait. The tension with patience is found in that moment of choice to wait for something or not to wait. I'd like to explore waiting on God's timing as well as being patient with others in our relationships. Understanding these two areas will help bring clarity to our minds when we face the tension of our choices.

- **Waiting on God's Timing** – How do you handle delays in your prayers? Perhaps you've been praying for a spouse, a deeply longed-for baby, a house, or a job you've been working toward. Why isn't it here? You prayed in faith and put everything in place as expected. Why hasn't it arrived? God's answer to us is yes, no, or not yet. Waiting for a Yes when we receive a No or a Not Yet can impact our soul, mind, and heart. King Solomon once said, 'Hope deferred makes the heart grow sick, but desire fulfilled is a tree of life' (Proverbs 13:12 ESV). It is our attitude during the waiting that helps us to protect our souls from sickness.

  I know a young woman who was devout in her relationship with God; she engaged in Bible studies, served in the church, and surrounded herself with Christian friends. However, as she went through her twenties, she grew tired of waiting for God's choice for her husband. She eventually gave up waiting and moved in with someone she met who didn't believe in God. She became pregnant right away, but he wanted nothing to do with her or the baby. Now, she raises her baby alone. Her heart grew sick of waiting, and she missed God's best plan for her. God can bring so much beauty out of heartache like this; His redeeming love can restore her to His path of righteousness, but she walked the hard way because she didn't wait.

  Instead of allowing our hearts to become sick, we can wait and receive the promises of God during periods of tension. The prophet Isaiah teaches us that 'but those who hope in the Lord will renew their strength. They will soar on wings like eagles; they will run and not grow weary, they will walk and not be faint' (Isaiah 40:31 NIV). With this truth, we receive the following rewards from being patient:

1. Renewal of spiritual strength
2. Higher perspective
3. Gained physical strength

Isaiah also explains deeper insight and says, 'Therefore the Lord waits to be gracious to you, and therefore he exalts himself to show mercy to you. For the Lord is a God of justice; blessed are all those who wait for him' (Isaiah 30:18 ESV). God is also waiting to be gracious to you so that you may receive the full joy of what you desire. He intends to show mercy to you in response to your longing. He promises that those who wait for Him will be blessed because He is a God of justice. What a comforting word He shares with us.

- **Being Patient in Our Relationships** – Sometimes we want our loved ones to act the way we need and want them to behave. What they need seems obvious, yet their lives are not ours to control. It's as though the more we love, the more we want to make things right. However, when we let go of control, we can live in the patience of waiting for God to do His work, which will undoubtedly yield far more powerful outcomes in our loved ones' lives than any of our best efforts. Paul explains we should 'Be joyful in hope, patient in affliction, faithful in prayer' (Romans 12:12 NIV). When we can pray and hand our loved ones over to God, then during the waiting time of being patient, we can witness God using the trouble, pain, and problems to create a masterpiece of beauty, hope, and future.

Bearing with One Another in Love

These virtues Paul urges us to walk in are not independent of each other but build upon one another. Humility is necessary for gentleness, and gentleness underpins patience; together, they perfectly lead us to the aspiration of bearing with one another in love. As they build upon one another, they demonstrate the practical implementation of love. To bear with each other's weaknesses requires a grace rooted in our humility.

We know Jesus loved us enough in our weakness that, through His grace, He died for us. That love sustains us as we bear with one another through the many weaknesses we find in each other. Have you ever observed a parent raising a child with a severe disability and wondered how they manage it? Or how a grandmother cares for her husband, who suffers from memory loss? The answer is love, which flows through their humility, patience, and gentleness.

It is possible to bear with each other in love through forgiveness. I'm not condoning subjecting ourselves to abuse. However, to live with each other, both in their strengths and weaknesses, love and forgiveness are daily habits to abide by. When our decision to forgive does not align with our feelings of hurt, we forgive others out of our faith in God and obedience to His instructions. However, it is more profound to forgive not just from our minds and will, but from our hearts also. This forgiveness arises from love. To extend the grace we desire to receive and allow that grace to envelop the person in love is a forgiveness that originates from the heart.

God desires us to willingly shed the things that hinder our love. While hurt and resentment fuel anger and pride, casting off these burdens allows our hearts to flow in humility with the Holy Spirit's fruit of gentleness, patience, and love. Relinquishing anger and resentment is pivotal for relating to others in love. This is why our healthy heart checks are so helpful in shedding all that hinders our hearts from fully walking in love. Love, after all, is the very reason

Jesus died for us. We are to live, 'bearing with one another, and forgiving one another, if anyone has a complaint against another; even as Christ forgave you, so you also must do' (Colossians 3:13 NKJV).

Live with Unity and Peace

Our ability to function in unity and peace brings some surprising blessings. This passage provides insight into what unity and peace produce in the family of God.

> Behold, how good and how pleasant it is
> For brethren to dwell together in unity!
>
> It is like the precious oil upon the head,
> Running down on the beard,
> The beard of Aaron,
> Running down on the edge of his garments.
> It is like the dew of Hermon,
> Descending upon the mountains of Zion;
> For there the LORD commanded the blessing—
> Life forevermore.
>
> Psalm 133 NKJV

When we live in unity with one another, it is precious to God. It allows the oil of the Holy Spirit to saturate us as a community. The abundant image of oil flowing down the head and face symbolises God's church living in harmony, from the leaders to the members. The anointing of the Holy Spirit blesses, empowers, and enriches us. Although we each possess unique passions, gifts, skills, and desires, we can also live together with a shared devotion, as if we have one heart. When one heart is formed by a diversity of unique individuals, God commands His blessing upon the group. This blessing of His anointing brings direction, breakthrough, healing, and progress.

Our unity actually commands God's blessing when we lay down our pride for the sake of others in churches, workplaces, and families. It truly takes humility, gentleness, and patience to relinquish our first choice of how to do something in favour of someone else's preference. Yet Paul teaches us to 'Submit to one another out of reverence for Christ' (Ephesians 5:21 NIV). We know within the church or at home, we must lay our pride down to do this willingly. Whether it is our church leader, our spouse, a friend, or a family member, sometimes wisdom nudges us to submit to each other. When we do, God's anointing pours abundantly out of the unity and peace that this produces. Remember the words of Jesus, 'Every kingdom divided against itself is brought to desolation; and every city or house divided against itself will not stand' (Matthew 12:25 KJV). The cost of leading our lives with pride is too great a cost to pay, for it leads to ruin—ruined families, ruined churches, friendship groups, businesses, and governments. However, division is closed down, and its momentum is lost when we humble ourselves and intentionally seek unity. The blessing from this is peace in our daily lives, our interactions, and in our souls; this peace is the fruit of the Holy Spirit.

Speak Truth in Love

We live in a generation where truth and opinion seem difficult to separate. There is a sense that everyone is entitled to choose their truth, and this makes their opinion a fact everyone must adhere to. However, opinion does not have the power to set us free. Jesus addresses the topic of truth and its importance for us as believers. 'So

Jesus said to the Jews who had believed him, "If you abide in my word, you are truly my disciples, and you will know the truth, and the truth will set you free"' (John 8:31–32 ESV). Here, Jesus teaches that to be His disciples, we are required to abide in His Word, which we know as the Bible. As we abide, meaning to live in, we will have the discernment to know the truth. This truth found in the pages of our Bibles acts as a compass in our lives, guiding our decisions in day-to-day interactions and relationships. As we live in the Word of God, it sets us free from much of the deception we face in this generation.

Paul uses truth as one weapon we must wear as we stand firm against Satan's schemes. He shares, 'Stand firm then, with the belt of truth buckled around your waist, with the breastplate of righteousness in place' (Ephesians 6:14 NIV). It's interesting that placing the belt of truth holds up the breastplate of righteousness, revealing that living in truth enables us to walk in righteousness. We must apply the truth first to truly uphold righteousness in our lives.

We should never speak the Word of God to those around us without love. If we do, we turn people away from our message. Paul puts it like this: 'If I speak in the tongues of men or of angels, but do not have love, I am only a resounding gong or a clanging cymbal' (1 Corinthians 13:1 NIV). We must carry in our hearts the joy that the gospel of Christ is good news! 'And how can someone tell them if he is not sent? The Holy Writings say, "The feet of those who bring the good news are beautiful"' (Romans 10:15 NLV).

Just as we should be willing to share a message of truth in love with others, sometimes it is wise to receive a word of truth in love ourselves. This enables us to truly grow as disciples. It is immensely valuable to have someone willing to offer correction for our growth, especially when they do so out of love for us. The Bible has much to say about this, with numerous verses indicating the benefits of being corrected. If we allow people to speak into our lives with love, mentor us, and even rebuke us, we can grow and mature in our faith. 'For the moment, discipline seems painful rather than pleasant, but later it yields a harvest of peace and righteousness in those who have been trained by it' (Hebrews 12:11 ESV).

As you continue to grow as a disciple, your eyes will open to the people around you whom God is positioning you to disciple. As you go about doing this, be willing to share a well-rounded truth with them to encourage them, pray with them, highlight the potential you see in their lives, recognise their gifts, and offer correction to help develop them. Remember this amazing reminder as you speak the truth in love: 'And let us consider how we may spur one another on toward love and good deeds, not giving up meeting together, as some are in the habit of doing, but encouraging one another—and all the more as you see the Day approaching' (Hebrews 10:24–25 NIV).

Becoming More Like Christ as We Grow and Mature in Our Faith

Paul discusses growing as a disciple of Christ, warning us not to be like children in our faith, easily deceived by false teachings. Instead, he urges believers to mature in their faith and be transformed more and more into the likeness of Jesus. Growth in Christ is inspired by knowing Christ through His Word in the Bible.

Being transformed into the likeness of someone depends on knowing them and being transformed in their image. Through this, we uncover the nature, values, and behaviour of Christ. We learn how He meets, interacts with, and responds to God, people, Satan, and sin. It's not just in the New Testament gospels where we find Jesus; as we study the whole Bible, we discover Jesus is actually the Word, and every book points to Christ. If we're willing, our time reading the Bible can be a relational and rich discovery alongside the Holy Spirit. When we read the Bible with the Holy Spirit, we learn from God and receive what He is revealing to us; our reading turns into fellowship with God. God loves to reveal His heart, truth, and even mysteries to us as we read His Word. 'He reveals deep and hidden things; he knows what lies in darkness, and light dwells with him' (Daniel 2:22 NIV).

Pray

When we pray, we believe God can do what we cannot. Our hearts are reminded of God's greatness and connect with His sovereign power. We come to Him knowing when we are weak, He is strong. The sense of His presence and the answers to our prayers encourage and increase our faith, and we grow our awareness of God's limitless capacity.

Praying is simply conversing with God, which we can do in countless ways. Sometimes with words, sometimes with sounds, or with tears. We often begin by giving thanks and expressing gratitude, sharing our troubles at times, and asking for our needs as well as the needs of others. However, in any two-way conversation, there is also a need to listen and receive from the other person. One way God wants us to engage with Him is to be still and know He is God. David taught, 'Be still, and know that I am God; I will be exalted among the nations, I will be exalted in the earth' (Psalm 46:10 NKJV). This is when we receive from God. When I come to God and am still, intentionally quieting myself, I sense His presence. In this presence, my heart can worship God. During this time, He also fills me with whatever my soul is thirsty to receive. If I'm anxious, He fills me with peace; if I feel flat, He fills me with hope. During Jesus' ministry on earth, He told a Samaritan woman, 'But whoever drinks the water I give them will never thirst. Indeed, the water I give them will become in them a spring of water welling up to eternal life' (John 4:14 NIV). By His Holy Spirit, God strengthens us in prayer, and our relationship with God matures. We come to understand the character of God more intimately and realise how limitless His power and reach are.

Choosing to make Christian friends is another important way to mature in our faith. King Solomon, the wisest person who ever lived, said, 'As iron sharpens iron, so one person sharpens another' (Proverbs 27:17 NIV). This refers to the quality of character of the people who shape us. If we spend time around people of poor character, we will be influenced by their character. If we invest our time with people who possess noble qualities, such as iron, they will shape and sharpen us, resulting in our quality being of high value.

Grow and Mature in the Likeness of Christ

We were created to grow and mature in the likeness of Christ together as a group of believers. The Bible often refers to the corporate group of believers as the body of Christ. Finding a Bible study group to learn and grow with is a significant help to Christians in maturing their faith and becoming more like Christ. Paul spoke of the importance of meeting together as believers, 'not giving up meeting together, as some are in the habit of doing, but encouraging one another—and all the more as you see the Day approaching' (Hebrews 10:25 NIV). Meeting together means we shine together like a vibrant fire. As each person goes through the challenges of life, they do not fall to the side and grow cold. Instead, they stay encouraged in their faith as each person prays for, cares for, and encourages individuals, couples, and families.

I encourage every Christian to have someone in their life to learn from—a mentor they can meet with regularly. I have had a few different mentors throughout my life. For many years, I was mentored by a prayer leader who invited me to pray with her for others. She taught me throughout these years and answered my questions as I grew in my faith. She provided advice and shared her wisdom and insights. Additionally, she taught me about spiritual principles that addressed areas of bondage for the people we prayed for. I truly would not have grown in prayer without a mentor in this area; I'm very grateful for her intentional investment of time and patience in my learning journey. My current mentor has invested in my growth for several years, initially providing group mentorship in leadership, Bible reading, and preaching. He now continues to contact me, listen, and share wisdom during the highs and lows of my circumstances, consistently being someone I can turn to for questions and advice. People like these are invaluable and significantly impact the development of disciples for Jesus. Just as others invest in us, we must also be willing to mentor younger Christians and help them grow more and more into the likeness of Jesus.

One mark of a mature Christian is the security they have in their identity. They carry themselves in a way that does not attempt to prove anything. The longer you know them, the more you see them carry a gentle confidence. Even when accused, they are slow to defend themselves because they are not insecure. They wait to speak, and when they do, they share words of wisdom. They know who they are, but more importantly, they know whose they are: the child of the Most High God.

Build the Church up in Love

Jesus died not only for individuals but also for the church as a collective body of believers. His motivation was a deep love and affection for the church. Some churches become territorial and focus on growing their congregations or individual projects. It's easy to forget each church is part of something much bigger. It's very powerful for a town or region when individual churches come together to pray and share a unified love for the people in their wider area. Paul taught, 'Husbands, love your wives, just as Christ loved the church and gave himself up for her' (Ephesians 5:25 NIV). His love was not for one church but for the whole church as a collective body.

Mature Christians will show respect for the differences among various denominations and appreciate the different worship and prayer styles. They also recognise different expressions of faith practices between these denominations. With Jesus being at the heart of the church, we should cheer each other on and encourage one another in love and maturity. As a church, individuals become a collective 'one' in Christ. Our standing before God transcends the dividing line of earthly separations. Instead, we embrace the identity of Jesus, which is more important than previous identities that have separated us. This is why Paul told the Galatian church, who were struggling to accept that both Jews and non-Jews could receive the grace of God equally, 'There is neither Jew nor Gentile, neither slave nor free, nor is there male and female, for you are all one in Christ Jesus' (Galatians 3:28 NIV).

We build the church in love by serving within our home churches. Our spiritual gifts, as well as our unique skills, are incredibly precious and valuable for uplifting people. Whether it's greeting at the door, assisting in the car park, singing in the worship team, serving in the children's ministry, preaching, or any other activity, all these forms of service aim to strengthen the people, which ultimately builds the church. When we serve in love, we practice the humility, gentleness, and patience that enable us to extend grace to one another as we work with one heart in unity, fostering a high regard for Jesus' beloved church, for which He gave Himself up.

Chapter 8

Marriage

Much of what I have learned about marriage started with what not to do! I invested much of my energy in reacting to injustices. If only I had invested in understanding and patience; instead, I now understand how my words and behaviour were giving Satan license to take ground in our marriage. I wanted a close, loving marriage, yet so many days felt like a bumpy ride led by emotions. With insecurities and sensitivity to rejection, many of my triggers were pressed. A few years into our marriage, I met another mother who taught me this marriage-saving verse, 'Death and life are in the power of the tongue, and those who love it will eat its fruit' (Proverbs 18:21 ESV). I began to understand we will eat of the fruit of our words, the words we share will produce either life or death. This changed the way I spoke about my marriage, to and about my children, and about every part of life. It's not about lying; it's about choosing words that hold space for hope and life to flow.

I learned that words of wisdom bring healing, and it's never too late for God to heal what is broken. 'There is one whose rash words are like sword thrusts, but the tongue of the wise brings healing' (Proverbs 12:18 ESV). The words of the wise must also include prayer in marriage. It is the faithful prayers of husbands and wives that transform an ordinary marriage into an exciting adventure of faith with God.

Before we learned this crucial concept in my marriage, we lived by the consequences of futile words, many born from my concerns and anxieties. Many times, when my husband Phil was travelling overseas for work and I was a young mother, my heart was weighed down by fear and even resentment. I felt abandoned in the responsibility for our three young children. I noticed that shortly after Phil left, chaos would erupt at home. Frequently, our cars would break down, technology would malfunction, and the house would fall into disorder. My resentful words and attitude would create a crack for the enemy to come in. Instead of operating under the God-given authority of Christ, my heart filled with fear and resentment, making us vulnerable to Satan's schemes, leading to weeks of disorder until my husband returned. My eyes were unaware of the relationship between spiritual order and its connection to our natural life.

Understanding the spiritual and physical principles within a husband-and-wife relationship is vital for a family to thrive in God's blessings. The relationship between husband and wife is not only sacred and precious to God but also serves as a metaphor for the relationship between Christ and the church. God uses the earthly relationship of marriage to reveal much about spiritual order and relational strength.

The order of Christ loving the church, which He refers to as His bride (Revelation 19:7–10), reflects the commitment and devotion of a husband to a wife and the adoration and love of a bride for her husband. God's covenant promises to bless Abraham and his descendants and families on earth signify an ongoing promise to bless both the collective family of God and individual families. This has been His intention from the very beginning. Spiritual order is a vital means for Him to facilitate the flow of both generational blessings and new, unique blessings for individual families.

Husband and Wife Unity

Just as Christ and the church are unified, the unity of husband and wife on earth is essential for both God's purposes to operate within a marriage. Earlier, we read Jesus teaches His disciples about the dangers of disunity, 'Every kingdom divided against itself is brought to desolation, and every city or house divided against itself will not stand' (Matthew 12:25 NKJV). This verse also applies to marriage as Jesus teaches a key principle here about the power of unity for protection from the enemy. When the enemy sees a kingdom, city, or house divided against itself, he sees a free opportunity to disrupt, destroy, and bring down the area altogether. This is why the covenant promise of marriage must include a wise plan to ensure the enemy has no way to enter in the first place.

Having unity does not mean a husband and wife share identical opinions and perspectives. In fact, the differences in opinions and viewpoints make the union all the stronger. It's the capability and willingness of individuals to navigate these differences that determines whether unity is maintained. Ideally, the skills for managing these differences are learned long before we even meet our spouses. We can learn this from watching other couples who have grasped the strength that unity brings. It's never too late to learn to handle relationships in a Christ-honouring and spouse-honouring way. Paul shares with us, 'Be completely humble and gentle; be patient, bearing with one another in love. Make every effort to keep the unity of the Spirit through the bond of peace' (Ephesians 4:2–3 NIV).

It's essential to recognise our fight isn't only about what is obvious and right in front of us. Paul explains it to us like this: 'For our struggle is not against flesh and blood, but against the rulers, against the authorities, against the powers of this dark world and against the spiritual forces of evil in the heavenly realms' (Ephesians 6:12 NIV). While we may think we are arguing about buying a new car or paying off the mortgage, we may actually be dealing with the power of fear or deception working between and prompting division between a husband and wife.

My husband and I would often clash over where we should live. After the birth of our first child, we had outgrown our unit. My focus was on our growing family needing more space; I wanted spacious living areas and large bedrooms, while he was concerned with financial security and minimising risk. Our interactions with each other were fiery and intense, leading us on a constant emotional merry-go-round filled with frustration, insults, and exhausting, never-ending unresolved tension. Both perspectives were valid, stemming from what we each considered priorities. We could only find unity after genuinely hearing each other's feelings and valuing each other's concerns. When we framed the issue as something in front of us to bring solutions to, rather than dividing us from being unified, we eventually compromised and purchased a medium-sized home with lower financial risk, which we renovated ourselves. Our conflict was not about having different priorities; it was about failing to honour and support each other. Our hearts were misaligned, and the enemy exploited our weakness and lack of emotional loyalty and unity with each other.

When we understand the connection between spiritual principles and our physical reality, we must be deliberate in attending to these spiritual principles. By being diligent about spiritual order in our marriage, we protect the relationship itself, the environment, and the flow of grace in our interactions. Focusing on diligence in spiritual order in our marriages creates a safeguarded path for the daily nitty-gritty of family life.

When We Have Totally Different Perspectives

Try to be objective so that the issue is in front of you, not between you. While your emotions are valid, they should not lead your conversation. Paul explains the importance of this: 'My dear brothers and sisters, take note of this: Everyone should be quick to listen, slow to speak and slow to become angry, because human anger does not produce the righteousness that God desires' (James 1:19–20 NIV).

Explain to your spouse what you think they are trying to say. Ask them if you got that right or if there is anything else they want to add. Proverbs 4:7 tells us to 'Get wisdom. Though it costs all you have, get understanding' (NIV). The cost of listening to each other is that we need to resist interrupting with our thoughts, lay our pride down, and listen with an open heart, seeking to learn a new perspective with genuine understanding, even if we don't agree.

Consider why their perspective is important to them and why they see it this way. Apologise if you have been disrespectful in any way in hearing their perspective. Being the first one to apologise is a huge act of humility which invites healing into the conversation and radically changes the atmosphere.

Share your perspective clearly and respectfully, and ask your spouse to share what they understand you to be saying. If they have overlooked key points, reiterate the aspects you believe have not been acknowledged.

Brainstorm ways to find a compromise together that honours both of your perspectives. It's okay to disagree on a topic while maintaining unity of heart. The outcome is not as important as your mutual respect. If you can't agree on a solution right now, set a time to revisit the issue later. Use that time to pray, reflect, and seek God's creative solutions. If time is pressing, seek godly counsel from someone you both trust who is qualified to provide guidance on the matter.

Commitment to Love

Often, our emotions can lead us into sin. Following our immediate feelings leads to behaviours we would never choose on a logical level, especially when such behaviours cause us to break our commitments and introduce betrayal into our marriage relationship.

The balance of success relies on our choices, love, and commitment to God, as well as our love and commitment to our spouse, even when our emotions suggest otherwise. Our love, along with our fear of the Lord, must be stronger than our emotions. Our deep reverence for God's overall power serves as an anchor for our commitment to our spouse. This forms the foundational base from which wisdom can flow. These are the defining factors that enable husbands and wives to uphold their covenant promise of love to each other.

'But you, O Lord, are a God merciful and gracious, slow to anger and abounding in steadfast love and faithfulness' (Psalm 86:15 ESV). Where we have chosen to introduce betrayal into our marriages, regardless of the consequences, we must repent before God and to our spouse. Building a relationship on deception will not receive God's blessing. However, humility, gentleness, and love provide an invitation for the Holy Spirit to do a great work in our lives and marriages.

A Prayer for Marriage

Lord, I invite You into every part of our marriage. Thank You for Your steadfast love, that Your arm is not too short to save, nor Your ear too dull to hear (Isaiah 59:1). Please prompt the ears of our hearts to live in accordance with Your will and Your Word. May Your Holy

Spirit be free to move, heal, and build truth into our hearts and in every part of our marriage. I ask that love be foundational in our marriage, binding all other virtues in unity (Colossians 3:14–17). I speak order and unity into our marriage with Christ as our head, and with (me/my husband) to freely steward the leadership of our family (Ephesians 5:23). Lord, may we submit to one another (Ephesians 5:21) with Christ at the heart of our marriage. I believe Your unity commands a blessing (Psalm 113). We receive Your blessing, Your healing, and Your deliverance (Psalm 103:2–3).

Lord, where we have been living with envy and suspicious accusations, we repent. Where we have been operating in pride and stubbornness, we are sorry. Where we have failed to honour each other and acted in self-seeking ways, we repent. Where we have been hot-tempered and easily angered, we ask Your forgiveness. Where we have kept a record of wrongs as a list to accuse, it is with sorrow. Thank You that You are faithful and just to forgive us our sins and to cleanse us from all unrighteousness (1 John 1:9–10). We receive Your forgiveness now. Thank You, Lord, that You are with us, You strengthen us, help us, and uphold us with Your righteous hand (Isaiah 41:10). Please protect our coming and our going, protect us from the schemes of the enemy. We declare Your protection over our union, our family, our home, our work, and our finances. In every circumstance, You are our refuge and strength, our very present help in times of trouble and in every area of our marriage and life (Psalm 46:1).

May our marriage rejoice in the truth. Always protecting each other with loyalty and commitment, sincerely trusting, hoping, and patiently persevering through each trial we face (1 Corinthians 13:4–8). May Your joy be present and overflowing in our relationship. May the peace of Christ rule our hearts (Colossians 3:15), allowing us to live restored lives, encouraging and calling out the potential in each other You have placed inside us. May we live each day abiding in Your love and peace and serving You, caring deeply for the needs of each other in all tenderness and love.

Lord, for every area of our marriage that has become dormant, dead, and dull, I speak resurrection life and power (Romans 6:4). I ask that Your power would be at work to awaken emotional and physical intimacy. That we would rekindle the delight of our youth to live each day in the tender, compassionate love You made us for. Awaken our hearts to freely serve each other humbly in love (Galatians 5:13–14). I thank You, Lord, that You supply every need according to Your riches in glory in Christ Jesus (Philippians 4:19). That every good and perfect gift comes from above, coming down from You our Father (James 1:17). Lord, we receive Your grace that abounds in our marriage; we thank You for Your sufficiency in all areas of our marriage. Lord, You abound in every good work; we thank You and need You (2 Corinthians 9:8).

Chapter 9

Holy Spirit

Who Is the Holy Spirit?

The Holy Spirit is the third person of the Trinity, uniquely separate, yet also one with Father God and Jesus. Understanding the Holy Spirit as a person helps clarify His personality. We can discover this personality throughout Scripture, but we can also experience it on a personal level through everyday life within a relationship with the Holy Spirit. Scripture describes the following attributes of the Holy Spirit:

- Gives love (Romans 8:27)
- Gives life (John 6:63)
- Can be grieved (Ephesians 4:30)
- Counsels us (John 14:26)
- Comforts us (John 14:26)
- Teach and help us (John 14:26)
- Lives in believers (Romans 8:11)
- Searches to understand our hearts and prays for us (Romans 8:27)
- Is the truth (1 John 5:6)

- Shares the following gifts with believers: knowledge, wisdom, faith, healing, prophecy, discernment, and speaking and interpreting in tongues (1 Corinthians 12:7–11)
- Is an advocate for Jesus who testifies about Him (John 15:26)
- Is the only person who knows the thoughts of God (1 Corinthians 2:10–11)

Receiving the Holy Spirit

Reading the Old Testament, our understanding of the Holy Spirit may be shaped by our reading of the Major and Minor Prophets, sharing their Spirit-inspired messages with various kings. Or perhaps it was our reading of the Holy Spirit's presence at creation. However, after Jesus died, a shift occurred where the presence of the Holy Spirit became far more personal with Christians and no longer confined to the prophets. After the arrival of the Holy Spirit, Paul taught the church of Corinth that we, as Christians, are to be temples of the Holy Spirit, hosting the Holy Spirit inside us as dwelling places for Him to live. He taught, 'Do you not know that you are God's temple and that God's Spirit dwells in you?' (1 Corinthians 3:16 ESV). This requires us to receive the Holy Spirit, housing His ministry and power within us. This is not only for our benefit and relationship with God, but also for our families, our church, and the world.

Jesus spoke of this also, 'Very truly I tell you, no one can enter the kingdom of God unless they are born of water and the Spirit' (John 3:5 NIV). Different church denominations refer to the receiving of the Holy Spirit with a variety of different terminologies. Pentecostal churches may refer to this as the baptism of the Holy Spirit, and other denominations may refer to this as receiving the Holy Spirit. The phrase 'born again' will often refer to the moment someone experiences their conversion when accepting Jesus as their Lord and Saviour, with water baptisms symbolising the rebirth. However, Jesus, in this Scripture, refers to being born of the Spirit, which means receiving the Holy Spirit with a renewal and rebirth of our Spirit.

Jesus Receiving the Holy Spirit

Jesus experienced both His water baptism and receiving the Holy Spirit during the same event. 'As soon as Jesus was baptised, he went up out of the water. At that moment, heaven was opened, and he saw the Spirit of God descending like a dove and alighting on him. And a voice from heaven said, "This is my Son, whom I love; with him I am well pleased"' (Matthew 3:16–17 NIV). This was a pivotal moment with Father God publicly endorsing Jesus, along with His receiving the empowerment of the Holy Spirit. It marked the transition from Him displaying not only His humanity but also His divinity. After receiving the Holy Spirit, Jesus' encounters with people led to healings, miracles, casting out demons, and even resurrecting the dead, with lives and families transformed forevermore.

We see that both Jesus' ministry and subsequent church ministry were established through the filling and empowerment of the Holy Spirit. This serves as the biblical model of effective Christianity.

The Church Receiving the Holy Spirit at Pentecost

Receiving the Holy Spirit enables us to live in His empowerment. Jesus explained it like this to His disciples, 'But you will receive power when the Holy Spirit has come upon you; and you will be my witnesses in Jerusalem and all Judea and Samaria, and to the end of the earth' (Acts 1:8 NIV). For the disciples to carry out their assignment, they required an empowerment they couldn't find in their natural state. Jesus was commissioning them to go and make more disciples, which would require Holy Spirit-empowered dreams, prophetic visions, healing, discernment, and even signs and wonders. These abilities extend far beyond the natural skills humans possess. The creation of the early church was far from a naturally formed institution. Instead, it was launched by the Holy Spirit's arrival.

Two weeks after Jesus informed His disciples they would receive the Holy Spirit; the Spirit arrived as a fire and a wind while the disciples were praying. As they were filled with the Holy Spirit, it granted them empowered speech, serving as a witness to nonbelievers: 'All of them were filled with the Holy Spirit and began to speak in other tongues as the Spirit enabled them' (Acts 2:4 NIV). Many observers who heard their native tongue being spoken, along with a Spirit-filled message from Peter, became converts. At that moment, the church was launched.

Peter, who had been commissioned by God to lead the early church, preached the first Christian sermon. Those who heard were 'cut to the heart' and asked what they should do. Peter replied, 'Repent and be baptised every one of you in the name of Jesus Christ for the forgiveness of your sins, and you will receive the gift of the Holy Spirit' (Acts 2:38 ESV).

In that moment, the church was propelled by the arrival of the empowerment of the Holy Spirit.

It may be tempting to view this Christian conversion as relevant only to those who were present, but Peter clarifies by saying, 'For the promise is for you and for your children and for all who are far off, everyone whom the Lord our God calls to himself' (Acts 2:39 ESV). This means we who weren't there that day are included in the message of hope to repent, be baptised, and receive the gift of the Holy Spirit.

Today's Christians continue the multiplication of disciples. As we grow, we will also begin to go and make more disciples. This is not something we can accomplish in our own strength; rather, we need the empowerment and gifts of the Holy Spirit to be effective disciple-makers. Each of us has a different role in how we make disciples, but disciple-making is for everyone.

Individuals Continuing to Receive the Holy Spirit by the Laying of Hands

After receiving the Holy Spirit at Pentecost, believers continued to multiply rapidly. Not only were Jews added to the believers, but also Samaritans (of Jewish Heritage) and Gentiles (non-Jews). Many new believers were not present at Pentecost. They had been baptised with water but had not yet been empowered by the Holy Spirit. Peter, John, and later Paul recognised this as leaders within the fast-growing church. In response, they were willing to lay hands on new believers to receive the filling of the Holy Spirit, thereby releasing the power of the Holy Spirit to them.

An example of the Holy Spirit being received through the laying of hands is in the book of Acts, where Paul was travelling through a region and encountered some disciples. He inquired whether they had received the Holy Spirit. Although they had been baptised in water, they had not received the Holy Spirit. So, Paul laid hands on them.

And it happened, while Apollos was at Corinth, that Paul, having passed through the upper regions, came to Ephesus. And finding some disciples, he said to them, "Did you receive the Holy Spirit when you believed?" So, they said to him, "We have not so much as heard whether there is a Holy Spirit." And he said to them, "Into what then were you baptised?" So, they said, "Into John's baptism." Then Paul said, "John indeed baptised with a baptism of repentance, saying to the people that they should believe on Him who would come after him, that is, on Christ Jesus." When they heard this, they were baptised in the name of the Lord Jesus. And when Paul had laid hands on them, the Holy Spirit came upon them, and they spoke with tongues and prophesied.

Acts 19:1-6 NKJV

The consequence of the Holy Spirit's power in them was they operated in the gifts of the Holy Spirit, delivering prophetic words and speaking in tongues. Even today, it is not unusual for people to speak in tongues when they receive the Holy Spirit.

Similarly, Peter and John were also laying hands on new disciples for the empowerment of the Holy Spirit.

When the apostles in Jerusalem heard that Samaria had accepted the Word of God, they sent Peter and John to Samaria. When they arrived, they prayed for the new believers there so that they might receive the Holy Spirit, because the Holy Spirit had not yet come on any of them. Before then, they had simply been baptised in the name of the Lord Jesus. Then Peter and John placed their hands on them, and they received the Holy Spirit. When Simon saw that the Spirit was given at the laying on of the apostles' hands, he offered them money and said, "Give me also this ability so that everyone on whom I lay my hands may receive the Holy Spirit." Peter answered: "May your money perish with you, because you thought you could buy the gift of God with money!"

Acts 8:14–20 NIV

Following the biblical model of receiving the Holy Spirit, many of us will ask our church leaders to lay hands and pray for our receiving of the Holy Spirit. While some people receive the empowerment of the Holy Spirit during their water baptism, just as Jesus did. We need to be open and alert to the Holy Spirit and receptive to the steps we can take to ensure the Holy Spirit is welcomed for the empowerment of His work in and through us.

Speaking in Tongues

We often offer prayers inspired by the Holy Spirit, especially when we feel compelled to pray for someone or a specific issue, sensing a burden to address their needs. We express these prayers in the language we typically use. The apostle Paul points out that Christians can use either the tongues of humans or the tongues of angels, which we refer to as *tongues*: 'If I speak in the tongues of men or of angels, but do not have love, I am only a resounding gong or a clanging cymbal' (1 Corinthians 13:1 NIV). He emphasises that regardless of the language in which we pray, we should keep love at the forefront of our speech and prayers.

Tongues for Intercession for Ourselves and Others

The gift of tongues, our heavenly language, is uniquely different from our usual language. Tongues is a language we do not generally use; instead, it is a heavenly language given by the Holy Spirit. 'Follow the way of love and eagerly desire gifts of the Spirit, especially prophecy. For anyone who speaks in a tongue does not speak to people but to God. Indeed, no one understands them; they utter mysteries by the Spirit' (1 Corinthians 14:1–2 NIV).

Those who speak in tongues have 'had the Holy Spirit come on them' and have allowed the Holy Spirit to express empowered speech through their mouths. There is a willingness to participate in the speaking of tongues; despite the sounds being unfamiliar, we choose to project our voices and move our mouths, even though we don't select the words and sounds we form.

'But you, dear friends, by building yourselves up in your most holy faith and praying in the Holy Spirit' (Jude 1:20 NIV). We build ourselves up by reading Scripture and being strengthened in faith as we trust God in our daily lives. But we also build ourselves up in faith by praying in the Holy Spirit. Paul said, 'I pray that out of his glorious riches he may strengthen you with power through his Spirit in your inner being' (Ephesians 3:16 NIV). This is exactly what speaking in tongues does for our inner being; it builds us up in strength. By praying in this way, we relinquish our normal speech for the empowered language that comes from the Holy Spirit. We might feel silly mentally, but in faith and humility, we release the prayers the Holy Spirit provides. As the Spirit searches our hearts, He guides our prayers, directing us to pray for what is truly needed. This is why, after we have prayed in tongues, it often feels like a burden has been lifted. It is also why we frequently receive prompts and ideas that lie outside our usual patterns of thinking. These ideas resonate within us through the prompting of the Holy Spirit. We receive deep revelations about God, ourselves, and the prayer needs of others when we pray in the Holy Spirit.

Tongues for Building up the Church

The public use of tongues during church services can encourage the church if someone present has the gift of interpreting tongues. When prayer is empowered by the Holy Spirit through tongues, church leaders may ask someone who has demonstrated the gift of interpreting to share the message of the prayer before the service continues. 'Anyone who speaks in a tongue edifies themselves, but the one who prophesies edifies the church. I would like every one of you to speak in tongues, but I would rather have you prophesy. The one who prophesies is greater than the one who speaks in tongues, unless someone interprets, so that the church may be edified' (1 Corinthians 14:4–5 NIV).

Not every church service employs this gift, as some may prefer to maintain a more orderly service. Do not be concerned if you are in a church and hear someone nearby praying in tongues during worship or a prayer gathering. They simply connect with the Holy Spirit and seek God's guidance in their prayers. If someone is sharing a public prayer for the church in tongues, then this prayer should be interpreted by someone with the gift of interpretation.

Tongues as a Sign for Unbelievers

Tongues are typically unknown sounds of unstructured and unofficial language; they can also be discernible languages we have never learned before speaking them. During these instances, for nonbelievers witnessing tongues, it has served as a sign of God's supernatural activity. 'Tongues, then, are a sign, not for believers but for unbelievers; prophecy, however, is not for unbelievers but for believers' (1 Corinthians 14:22 NIV). This is because tongues are sometimes expressed in languages of other nations. There are many testimonies of individuals praying in languages they have never learned. For those hearing these tongues, it serves as evidence God operates beyond the natural. 'When they heard this sound, a crowd came together in bewilderment, because each one heard their own language being spoken. Utterly amazed, they asked: "Aren't all these who are speaking Galileans? Then how is it that each of us hears them in our native language?"' (Acts 2:6–8 NIV). It is amazing the impact that this has made on the building of the church at Pentecost. 'Both Jews and converts to Judaism; Cretans and Arabs—we hear them declaring the wonders of God in our own tongues!' (Acts 2:11 NIV). It really shows us how dynamic the Holy Spirit is. We can never underestimate the power and reach of the Holy Spirit.

Living with the Holy Spirit

Living with the Holy Spirit allows us to access many of God's virtues. Through our intimate relationship with God's Spirit, He grants us access to these out of the pleasure of His relationship with us. Paul shares with us exactly what the Holy Spirit allows us to receive. 'But the fruit of the Spirit is love, joy, peace, forbearance, kindness, goodness, faithfulness, gentleness, and self-control. Against such things there is no law' (Galatians 5:22–23 NIV). These fruits of the Holy Spirit are not only received during our quiet times with God but also from the grace granted to us during times of challenges, relationship dilemmas, and trials.

At times, the Holy Spirit can prompt people to speak into our lives and meet our needs according to His guidance. Several years ago, my family was confronted with the sudden news that my father had been diagnosed with aggressive cancer. We were all very shocked by the news, as we had not heard any reports of symptoms leading up to it. Concern nagged at my heart, and I felt unsettled by the diagnosis. About a week after receiving this news, early one morning, I experienced a dream in which God handed me a rolled-up note to take from His hand. The note contained a Bible verse that brought me deep comfort. Immediately after the dream, I woke up, sat in bed, and contemplated the Bible verse I could not remember having read before. A text message from a lady in my church interrupted my thoughts. When I opened the message, it contained the exact Bible verse I had just received in my dream. The lady wrote the verse and said she felt prompted to send it to me regarding my father's cancer diagnosis. The experience was incredibly encouraging, as the Holy Spirit had worked in my dream to assure me of God's hand in my father's situation, and the Holy Spirit had also prompted the lady in my church, who responded in obedience by texting it to me. The doctors provided medical treatment, but they were surprised when, only six months after my father's cancer diagnosis, he was declared cancer-free.

For me, dreams have often served as a way for the Holy Spirit to reveal God's heart to me. Perhaps I talk too much to listen while I'm awake, and dreams provide moments when I'm quiet enough for God to reach me.

Living with the Holy Spirit means we stay open to whatever promptings the Spirit gives us. A certain person may frequently come to our mind or heart; often, this is the Holy Spirit prompting us to contact and encourage them. We might have plans for the day, but sense the Holy Spirit is nudging us to rearrange those plans, and only afterwards do we understand why. I remember my mother waking up in the night with a strong urge to pray for my brother, seeking God's protection for him. Thankfully, she was obedient to this prompting, as it was during this time that my brother was involved in a serious car accident. Thankfully, his injuries were minimal, reminding us of our need to live life with the Holy Spirit.

Chapter 10

Healing

The topic of healing should not be made into a complicated theology. Jesus taught that entering the kingdom of heaven requires a childlike faith (Matthew 18:24). As we receive our kingdom inheritance on earth, we also do so with a simple childlike faith. When we trust how good our Father God really is, it makes it natural to simply ask and receive as a child would ask their Father. In the same way, we should approach our prayers for healing with a simple childlike faith.

Jesus' Death Provides Forgiveness and Healing

On multiple occasions, the Bible refers to both our healing and forgiveness found in the grace given by His death and resurrection. For example, Psalm 103 offers insight into how this really works. It teaches us the breadth of what our redemption offers, describing precisely what we are redeemed from. This psalm highlights that by Jesus' death, He 'forgives all your sins and heals all your diseases, who redeems your life from the pit and crowns you with compassion' (v 3–4 NIV). The vital component here is the willingness of Christ to die, the offering of Christ made by God the Father, and our willingness to confess our sins and receive our personal redemption, healing, and compassion. To live each day in the saving grace of Jesus is to live each day with repentant hearts before the Lord, but also to actively embrace the saving grace of His healing.

When Jesus healed the paralytic, which we read in Matthew 9:1–8, Mark 2:1–12, and Luke 5:17–26, His words revealed valuable insight into His desire to offer forgiveness and healing. "'Which is easier: to say, 'Your sins are forgiven,' or to say, 'Get up and walk'? But I want you to know that the Son of Man has authority on earth to forgive sins." So he said to the paralysed man, 'Get up, take your mat and go home' (Matthew 9:5–6 NIV). For Christ's full gift to us is our redemption from sin and sickness. This act of forgiveness and healing for humanity before His death foreshadowed His ultimate ministry of redemption from sin and sickness.

The Past, Present, and Future Tense of Our Healing

With the timing of our healing, we shouldn't view its timing as merely linear and moving forward. The Bible teaches that every healing we receive has been granted in the past, yet it is indeed available now, but it also refers to our future healed state in heaven.

First Peter 2:24 describes that we were healed with the past tense '"He himself bore our sins" in his body on the cross, so that we might die to sins and live for righteousness; "by his wounds you have been healed"' (NIV). All the healing we received is because of what Jesus has already done for us. Similarly, our acceptance into heaven is based on the forgiveness received through Christ on the cross.

The reason some people do not receive their healing on earth now is a mystery, yet this does not negate the fact the promise of our healing is secure, although it extends beyond our earthly dimension of time. For in heaven, the healed state is for all. The apostle John explains, 'He will wipe away every tear from their eyes, and death shall be no more, neither shall there be mourning, nor crying, nor pain be any more' (Revelation 21:4 ESV). Even though some are still seeking their healing on earth, we can confidently pray to release healing, knowing we will see it either now or in heaven, because the price for our healing has already been paid and given.

Words, Faith, and Belief

Earlier in the book, on the topic of marriage, I mentioned the importance of our words. This is also a crucial truth in being intentional about our healing. King Solomon, whom the Bible acknowledged as the wisest man to ever live, imparted important insights into the power of our words through his wisdom. Regarding our words, because it's such a key, we read again, 'The tongue has the power of life and death, and those who love it will eat its fruit' (Proverbs 18:21 NIV). The power of speaking is first seen in Genesis when God spoke the world into creation. Each day, He spoke a pronouncement for that which He created.

Being made in His image, we can also create with our words. This principle is seen when we read of Ezekiel, who prophesied over a valley of piles of dead bones, and miraculously, his words ignited life back into those dry bones. This resulted in a vast army of living people with flesh on their bones and air in their lungs (Ezekiel 37:1-14). The principle also works in a negative sense when speaking words of death by forming agreements with Satan's powers of fear and destruction. For example, if we speak curses about ourselves, such as 'I'm always sick, I'm always tired, I'm always having accidents,' then our words act like a rudder, steering our lives in the direction we declare. Those who make declarations like this see their lives affected by the bad fruit of their words.

In contrast, Jesus actively demonstrated the power of our words, faith, and belief regarding physical breakthroughs. While walking with His friends, He cursed a fig tree. The next day, they noticed it had withered from the roots. Jesus replied: '"Have faith in God," he answered... "if anyone says to this mountain, 'Go, throw yourself into the sea,' and does not doubt in their heart but believes that what they say will happen, it will be done for them"' (Mark 11:22–23 NIV).

Can you imagine how powerful this lesson must have been, standing beside the withered tree, as the disciples saw Jesus was sharing a true principle of prayer with them to activate powerful breakthroughs? Jesus explained further, 'Therefore I tell you, whatever you ask for in prayer, believe that you have received it, and it will be yours' (Mark 11:24 NIV).

The instruction is clear that Jesus is asking for bold prayers of faith. Instead of merely asking for it, He instructs us to speak to the obstacle and command it be moved.

What He shares next is a critical key we must follow for our prayer to flow in purity. 'And when you stand praying, if you hold anything against anyone, forgive them, so that your Father in heaven may forgive you your sins' (Mark 11:25 NIV). We must not overlook this step of humbling ourselves by forgiving those who have hurt us so that we can pray with a clear heart.

The speed at which the fig tree withered in just one day illustrates we can speak to sickness in faith and witness it wither quickly. Our words naturally flow from our beliefs, which come from our hearts, serving as our belief centre. Jesus addressed the significance of our words when speaking to the Pharisees, who condemned Him with their words. Jesus said, 'For out of the abundance of the heart the mouth speaks' (Matthew 12:34 RSV). This emphasises the importance of taking every measure to protect our hearts, as the condition of our heart influences what we say and impacts our entire lives. 'Above all else, guard your heart, for everything you do flows from it' (Proverbs 4:23 NIV).

Personal Healing Declaration

Heal me, O' Lord, and I will be healed (Jeremiah 17:14). I receive Your healing, Father. I live each day and each moment in the healing You have gifted to me. Your healing deeply reaches every part of my body as a perfect gift from above, coming from Your perfect plan (1 Peter 2:24)

I receive Your power that strengthens me now. It pours forth out of the abundant overflow of Your glorious riches. It satisfies. Your power brings energy and life to my body. I am strengthened in my body and mind through Your Spirit (Ephesians 3:16). I soak in Your presence and am filled with the power and strength that comes from Your Spirit flowing deeply inside every cell and every organ, through my blood, and into my bones.

I declare full faith in You and the sacrifice of Your Son, Jesus, as a redemption and release of my sin and my sickness. Thank You that Jesus took up my infirmities and carried my sorrows, allowing Himself to be stricken and struck down for my healing, my life, and my wholeness (Isaiah 53:4). I Incline my ears to Your words and keep them in my heart, for they are life to my body and health to my flesh (Proverbs 4:20–22). I meditate on Your words and believe in full confidence they are true for me. You sent Your Word to heal me (Psalm 107:20). I choose as an act of my will to live by faith in You, in Your Word, and in Your promises. I commit to You the words of Jeremiah: 'Heal me, Lord, and I will be healed.' For I believe healing is my inheritance, as I am an heir with Christ Jesus.

You are the resurrection and the life, and I receive a full measure of resurrection life and health into my whole body, including my brain, heart, organs, cells, genes, skin, lungs, respiratory system, muscles, tendons, and immune system. Your presence fills every part of me, and in You, I am complete. Thank You, Lord, that every good gift of health and healing is perfect from above, coming from You, my Father.

Chapter 11

Deliverance

Deliverance can be one of those topics that isn't often discussed. Yet for family members who urgently need deliverance, finding answers is essential. The best way to learn about how deliverance works is to learn from Jesus' ministry in this area as well as from the many examples found throughout broader Scripture

What Is Deliverance?

Understanding the authority we can use to break free from the powers of darkness is best approached with preparation. When examining Jesus' instructions on deliverance, there is a surprising synergy with preaching, healing, and deliverance that Jesus commanded simultaneously. Whether deliverance is sought for you or for your spouse, child, or an extended family member, it is not only possible but also a part of our inheritance as believers. Deliverance is very much a part of the freedom package Jesus invites us to partake in. It is also an essential spiritual weapon for us as family members caring for one another.

To be delivered means being rescued or set free. Our freedom, both corporately and personally, was the pinnacle goal of Jesus' life and ministry: 'it is for freedom that Christ has set us free' (Galatians 5:1 NIV).

God compares the deliverance of the nation of Judah to the delivery of a child during childbirth (Isaiah 66:7–9). He describes the labour pains that lead a woman to the moment of delivery. Likewise, we often endure a painful process leading up to our own deliverance, and it is the intense symptoms of our struggles that drive us to recognise our need for salvation. Just as Judah's deliverance as a nation represents rebirth, our personal deliverance also brings about a new beginning, allowing us to live a life free from ties to the enemy while embracing life in Christ's freedom. Deliverance provides hope for a future filled with the blessed promises of God as Abraham's descendants and as sons and daughters of God.

We have examined deliverance with the broad concept of the nation of Judah, but lets zoom in closer to the individual examples of deliverance in the Old Testament.

We read that Daniel was supernaturally delivered from the attack of lions. He was again rescued along with his friends from the fiery furnace. In these instances, God would not allow the consequences of the evil judgment of earthly authority to hinder the protection of His people. He saved Jonah from the grip of a whale, demonstrating the powers of nature were no match for the power of God. Defying all odds, the Philistine giant Goliath could not defeat Israel's army, as God sent David as an instrument of deliverance. The Israelites were saved from the perils of the Red Sea and instead crossed on safe ground. There are countless examples in the Old Testament to mention, but the point is clear: God is the deliverer of His people.

On a corporate level, God's grand gesture of deliverance for His people was offered by the gift of His Son, Jesus, who was a willing instrument of grace for our deliverance. Because of Jesus' death, we received our greatest deliverance of all, our salvation. Being delivered from darkness into his glorious light.

After receiving the Holy Spirit, Jesus frequently cast out demons from those who were afflicted. Whilst at the synagogue, Jesus shared His messianic assignment and revealed that His ministry purpose was to set the oppressed free. He shared Isaiah's prophecy from seven hundred years prior 'The Spirit of the Lord is on me, because he has anointed me to proclaim good news to the poor. He has sent me to proclaim freedom for the prisoners and recovery of sight for the blind, to set the oppressed free' (Luke 4:18 NIV). He publicly announced His ministry of deliverance as being the fulfilment of Isaiah's prophecy. God's deliverance is not only corporate, but He also engages in deliverance on a personal level for individuals.

I find it motivating yet also confronting that before Jesus ascended into heaven, He delegated to us as believers, the responsibility of casting out demons. He instructed that we will do so in the authority of His name. 'And these signs will accompany those who believe; In my name they will drive out demons; they will speak in new tongues' (Mark 16:17 NIV). All authority in heaven and earth has been given to us by Jesus (Matthew 28:18). The timing of Him leaving this responsibility with us aligns with the timing of His leaving the Holy Spirit with us. There is such a close connection between deliverance and the Holy Spirit. It's vital that we engage in prayers of deliverance with the Holy Spirit, as this allows us to discern how to approach the prayer. It's also important to speak the name of Jesus during our time of ministry. It's the tandem power of Jesus, together with the Holy Spirit and our willingness to pray for the oppressed, that works mightily to release people from the power of darkness.

Personal Deliverance From Evil Spirits

While we have looked at deliverance on a corporate level, it is important to consider deliverance is often needed on an individual level. Churches often refer to the process of being set free from evil spirits as 'deliverance' or 'deliverance ministry'. The notion of personal deliverance is not referring to being rescued in a general sense but more specifically being rescued from the influences of one or more evil spirits. Our personal deliverance, is enabled by Jesus who prioritised the practice of casting out evil spirits during his ministry on earth. He also instructed believers to pray for those afflicted by evil spirits (Mark 16:17).

Some Common Ways People Experience Deliverance

Deliverance can come through worship, a spoken word, and prayer. For example:

- **Individual Prayer Ministry** - This can be arranged by booking an appointment at a church with experienced prayer leaders. These specific prayers address areas of spiritual bondage. The prayer person, known as an intercessor, will likely ask you questions about any traumatic or occult experiences you may have had, read Scriptures, and pray for the breaking of bondage.
- **Church Services** - As people embrace the worship songs they are singing and sermon messages they are hearing, their will emerges to resist the enemy's power as they turn towards God's truth. This is often a gentle deliverance that the recipient may not even notice. 'Resist the devil and he will flee from you' (James 4:7).

We read of Jesus' intentional approach to personal deliverance as He encountered a demon-possessed man as He goes about ministering one day.

'When evening came, many who were demon-possessed were brought to him, and he drove out the spirits with a word and healed all the sick' (Matthew 8:16 NIV). When Jesus asked His disciples to preach the gospel, He would also instruct them to heal the sick and cast out demons. Essentially, a deep encounter with the Holy Spirit carries the resurrection power to open hearts to receive the gospel, attain healing, and be delivered from oppression. As Christian disciples, we don't serve a measly God, but a God who desires our complete freedom.

Jesus Casts out Evil Spirits Below, I have included some examples of Jesus delivering people from demonic powers. It's important that we learn from Jesus' example for our own involvement in receiving deliverance and, at times, being used by God to pray for the deliverance of others. Let's first look at Mark 5:1–20.

A Man Named Legion

They went across the lake to the region of the Gerasenes. When Jesus got out of the boat, a man with an impure spirit came from the tombs to meet him. This man lived in the tombs, and no one could bind him anymore, not even with a chain. For he had often been chained hand and foot, but he tore the chains apart and broke the irons on his feet. No one was strong enough to subdue him. Night and day among the tombs and in the hills he would cry out and cut himself with stones.

When he saw Jesus from a distance, he ran and fell on his knees in front of him. He shouted at the top of his voice, "What do you want with me, Jesus, Son of the Most High God? In God's name don't torture me!" For Jesus had said to him, "Come out of this man, you impure spirit!"

Then Jesus asked him, "What is your name?"

"My name is Legion," he replied, "for we are many." And he begged Jesus again and again not to send them out of the area.

A large herd of pigs was feeding on the nearby hillside. The demons begged Jesus, "Send us among the pigs; allow us to go into them." He gave them permission, and the impure spirits came out and went into the pigs. The herd, about two thousand in number, rushed down the steep bank into the lake and were drowned.

Those tending the pigs ran off and reported this in the town and countryside, and the people went out to see what had happened. When they came to Jesus, they saw the man who had been possessed by the legion of demons, sitting there, dressed and in his right mind; and they were afraid. Those who had seen it told the people what had happened to the demon-possessed man—and told about the pigs as well. Then the people began to plead with Jesus to leave their region.

As Jesus was getting into the boat, the man who had been demon-possessed begged to go with him. Jesus did not let him, but said, "Go home to your own people and tell them how much the Lord has done for you, and how he has had mercy on you." So the man went away and began to tell in the Decapolis how much Jesus had done for him. And all the people were amazed.

Mark 5:1–20 NIV

When the possessed man saw Jesus, he ran over to Him and fell on his knees.

The possessed man instinctively knew Jesus carried the power to help him. When we seek deliverance, we should pursue Christians filled with the Holy Spirit. Even Jesus did not operate in deliverance ministry until He had received the Holy Spirit. Certain churches have prayer team members who possess years of experience in this type of prayer and work closely with the Holy Spirit to discern the specific prayers for each individual they pray for.

At times, individuals affected by the demonic may have both a spiritual and physical reaction to God's presence. Don't be alarmed if you observe or experience an unsettled reaction, which may include agitation, physical outbursts, and disruptive behaviour, particularly when the Holy Spirit is at work during prayer ministry sessions. This can indicate deliverance may be near, as demonic influences are being stirred. In this initial interaction, the individual praying for someone who is oppressed will discern and assess the situation.

Jesus' response after His initial interaction with the possessed man was to take authority by commanding the impure spirits to leave him. (v 8).

Prayer team members will take authority over bondage and seek insight from the Holy Spirit while considering the symptoms of the individual they are praying for. This may involve asking thoughtful questions and paying attention to actions that could provide insights regarding the person's symptoms.

The symptoms of the demon-possessed man in Mark 5:1–20 were:

- supernatural strength that could even break chains
- isolation, as people were not safe to interact with him
- torment day and night (emotional and physical)
- cutting, self-harm

The man begged not to be tortured by Jesus because he recognised the authority of Jesus, calling Him the 'Son of Most High.' As you interact with a person needing deliverance, they will also be aware of what authority you are operating in because our positioning is established in the spirit. Jesus was positioned as Son of the Most High, and we are operating in the authority of Christ that He allocated to us to 'cast out all demons' (Luke 9:1 NLT). We communicate that authority when we speak the name of Jesus out loud and read out some Scriptures to assert His authority into the environment.

Jesus used His authority to cast the demons into the herd of pigs, for them to drown in the sea. He was confident and clear with the demons, simply permitting them to go. This confidence and clear instructions are important for us too. Allow our instruction to be clear, with an expectation of obedience for every evil spirit.

Jesus asked the man to share with the town, declaring first how much He had done for him and second, how the Lord had mercy on him. The result of the man's deliverance was that the townspeople were amazed. Those close to people who have not yet been delivered can observe the true freedom and dramatic contrast. The life of the delivered person serves as a powerful testimony for all who witness their struggles. This passage teaches us Jesus restored this man to his right mind and dignity, which likely led to restored relationships. We are His instruments, and our obedience allows us to confidently work with authority to cast out the demons of those who are oppressed. Let's not miss the opportunity to share what God has done for us and to testify to His mercy in our transformed lives. These testimonies point to God's glory and encourage others to seek their own freedom.

A Terrorised Son

> The next day, when they came down from the mountain, a large crowd met him. A man in the crowd called out, "Teacher, I beg you to look at my son, for he is my only child. A spirit seizes him and he suddenly screams; it throws him into convulsions so that he foams at the mouth. It scarcely ever leaves him and is destroying him. I begged your disciples to drive it out, but they could not",
>
> Luke 9:37–40 NIV (Also see Mark 9:14–29/Matthew 17:14–20.)

In the chapter before this deliverance, we read of the transfiguration Jesus experienced; we see Jesus has an intense interaction with the radiance and glory of God. There is an interesting transition we observe between two sequential gospel stories. We may expect such an exhilarating supernatural encounter would lead to any number of holy events. Yet immediately after this, He faced the urgent encounter with the powers of Satan, dramatically at work in a young family's life. Even when we are walking closely with God and having glorious encounters with Him, we are not immune to the works of Satan around us. The boy's distressed father came to Jesus and begged Him to look at his young son.

The information about his symptoms is presented to Jesus by his father as Jesus asks, 'How long has he been like this?' The demonic possession caused the following symptoms:

- a spirit caused seizure (distinctly different from a physiological seizure)
- distressed, crying out
- mute
- rigid
- gnashing teeth
- convulsions
- foaming mouth
- rapid and sudden spiritual departure
- bruising
- thrown into fire or water

It's notable the father seeking deliverance confessed his belief in the power of Jesus. The confession of our faith is a powerful way to break our alignment with the power of unclean spirits.

The father said, "'But if you can do anything, take pity on us and help us.' "If you can?" said Jesus. "Everything is possible for one who believes." Immediately, the boy's father exclaimed, "I do believe; help me overcome my unbelief!"' (Mark 9:22–24 NIV).

This father's faith, humility, and surrender to God are so important when seeking deliverance. Jesus' response was to set the man's son free from the unclean spirit. 'When Jesus saw that a crowd was running to the scene, he rebuked the impure spirit. "You deaf and mute spirit," he said, "I command you, come out of him and never enter him again"' (Mark 9:25 NIV).

Jesus did three things during the boy's deliverance:
1. Rebuked the impure spirit
2. He identified it as a deaf and mute spirit
3. He clearly commanded it to come out and further instructed it to never enter him again.

In doing this, Jesus reinstated the boy:
1. Into right health (sound body)
2. Dignity (sound mind)
3. Right relationship with his family (sound relationships)

Our deliverance from the affliction of impure spirits grants us freedom in our bodies and puts us in our right minds. The flow-on effect is healthy relationships. Jesus truly came to set the captives free. His instruction and intention are for us to continue the ministry of freedom by working closely with the Holy Spirit.

Before Jesus had arrived on the scene to offer this miracle of deliverance, the disciples had been trying to bring deliverance to the boy also, yet they, unlike Jesus, had not been successful. This confused them, so they asked Jesus privately about the matter. Jesus explained that prayer and fasting were necessary for this kind of deliverance. 'And when He had come into the house, His disciples asked Him privately, "Why could we not cast it out?" He replied, "This kind can come out only by prayer and fasting" (Mark 9:28–29 NKJV). Some demonic spirits are more powerful than others and require total reliance on the power of God through our surrender and weakness.

Chapter 12

Positioning Ourselves for Deliverance

Fasting

Fasting was the first thing Jesus did when He was filled with the Holy Spirit. He went into the desert, choosing to abstain from food for a staggering forty days. During this time, He was heavily tested by Satan, but it was His posture of submission, humility, and surrender before God that enabled Him to receive the strength to overcome every temptation Satan brought His way. Fasting is our way of surrendering our strength to receive God's strength because when we are weak, He is strong (2 Corinthians 12:9–10).

Humbling - We can approach fasting in several ways. Most commonly, it involves abstaining from food or following an altered diet for a short period. It serves to humble ourselves before God. When we refrain from eating, our bodies weaken, and our hearts naturally turn to God. During fasting periods, we witness God's strength and activity on our behalf as we starve pride and independence in our lives, creating space for dependence on Him. Jesus fasted for forty days in the desert before the official beginning of His ministry on earth. This practice is both modelled and taught to us, guiding our approach to fasting. It also conveys that fasting brings a reward:

'When you fast, do not look somber as the hypocrites do, for they disfigure their faces to show others they are fasting. Truly I tell you, they have received their reward in full. But when you fast, put oil on your head and wash your face, so that it will not be obvious to others that you are fasting, but only to your Father, who is unseen; and your Father, who sees what is done in secret, will reward you' (Matthew 6:16–18 NIV).

The reward of fasting certainly brings about a breakthrough in our spiritual lives, which subsequently affects our physical reality. This is why fasting is a powerful tool for seeking deliverance and healing. The reward, which is life-changing, flows from the deep relationship we cultivate with God.

'For those who exalt themselves will be humbled, and those who humble themselves will be exalted' (Matthew 23:12 NIV). Throughout Scripture, time and time again, we see God's heart for Israel moved in compassion when they humble themselves and turn to God. 'If my people, which are called by my name, shall humble themselves, and pray, and seek my face, and turn from their wicked ways; then will I hear from heaven, and will forgive their sin, and will heal their land' (2 Chronicles 7:14 KJV). For those seeking deliverance, fasting is a powerful way of weakening and humbling ourselves when seeking a powerful move of God. Common time periods for fasting are three days without food or seven, twenty-one, or forty days with partially abstaining from usual foods.

Deliverance - Jesus explained to His disciples that certain areas of deliverance require fasting for a breakthrough. 'This kind can come forth by nothing, but by prayer and fasting' (Mark 9:29 KJV). Jesus delivered people in various contexts, and He highlighted to His disciples that sometimes fasting is indeed the vital weapon needed. If you have been seeking deliverance and haven't seen your breakthrough, then fasting and prayer are your weapons of warfare. They break the yoke of oppression and set the oppressed free. Abstaining from injustice is an important aspect of fasting. We must be aware of not just food, but also our heart posture. We must love mercy and justice, striving for love while pursuing freedom. The grace and freedom offered to others aligns our hearts to receive grace and freedom from God. I really love how Isiah brings clarity to this. I feel my own heart moved with passion to see the outworking of this as I read his inspiring words in Isaiah 58:6–9 about fasting.

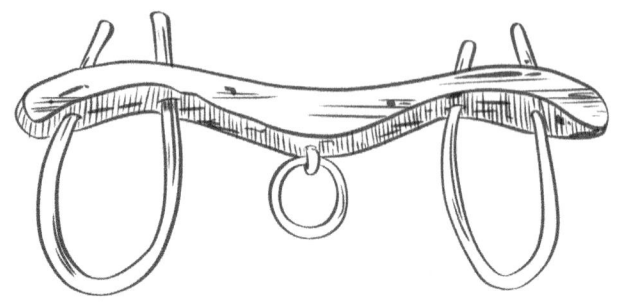

To live in fairness with others in right living and prayer

Is not this the kind of fasting I have chosen: to loose the chains of injustice and untie the cords of the yoke to set the oppressed free and break every yoke?

To care for the poor

Is it not to share your food with the hungry and to provide the poor wanderer with shelter—when you see the naked, to clothe them, and not to turn away from your own flesh and blood?

To live in revelation of the Holy Spirit

Then your light will break forth like the dawn, and your healing will quickly appear; then your righteousness will go before you, and the glory of the LORD will be your rear guard. Then you will call, and the LORD will answer; you will cry for help, and he will say: Here am I.

Isaiah 58:6–9 NIV

Fasting is a unique and special means of tuning into the plans of the Holy Spirit. Times of prayer and fasting allow us access to specific revelation regarding deliverance needs, with specific prompting guiding us to ask key questions, declare powerful Scriptures, and instigate prayer areas to pray into.

Fasting is also highly beneficial for the next steps towards freedom, which involve living the Christian life according to the revelation of the Holy Spirit's will. In the book of Acts, we see leaders in the early church were utilising prayer and fasting for ministry decisions and discerning God's calling for disciples. Prophets and teachers laid hands on Barnabas and Saul to commission them for the ministry based on the insight they gained from the Holy Spirit while praying and fasting:

> Now in the church at Antioch there were prophets and teachers: Barnabas, Simeon called Niger, Lucius of Cyrene, Manaen (who had been brought up with Herod the tetrarch) and Saul. While they were worshipping the Lord and fasting, the Holy Spirit said, "Set apart for me Barnabas and Saul for the work to which I have called them." So after they had fasted and prayed, they placed their hands on them and sent them off. The two of them, sent on their way by the Holy Spirit, went down to Seleucia and sailed from there to Cyprus.
>
> Acts 13:1–4 NIV

Pre-deliverance Preparation

I advise caution in approaching prayer for deliverance from evil spirits to Christians who have not first gone through the necessary steps of forgiveness. This is because unforgiveness gives the enemy a legal right to remain. Before praying for deliverance, address any legal rights the enemy currently holds. Declaring the name of Jesus and reading Scripture out loud prompts the enemy to flee. The pre-deliverance prayer below will guide you in forgiving those who have hurt you and renouncing sin in your life. Here are some prompts to consider before reading your pre-deliverance prayer.

Consider:

- What involvements have I had with the occult (occult practices, visits to fortune tellers, Ouija boards, curses, or other)?
- What involvement have I had with division in relationships (lies, false accusations, gossip, or others)?
- What unfair gains have I made from people and businesses (stealing, fraud, or other)?
- What sexual experiences have I engaged in that are outside of God's plans for me (fornication, perversion, porn)?
- Any other areas of sin

God did not come to condemn us but to save us and lead us into healthy relationships and living. We acknowledge and surrender our sins before God in recognition of our mistakes for Him to cleanse us by the blood of Jesus. 'For God did not send his Son into the world to condemn the world, but to save the world through him. Whoever believes in him is not condemned, but whoever does not believe stands condemned already because they have not believed in the name of God's one and only Son' (John 3:17–18 NIV).

Consider these steps prior to praying for deliverance.

The following four steps are included in the pre-deliverance prayer below as key elements.

1. Repentance
2. Forgiveness of others
3. Salvation
4. The power of reading Scripture out loud

Pre-deliverance Prayer

Lord, You have the power to take the burden from my shoulders and the yoke from my neck. I believe in faith that the yoke of my oppression shall be destroyed because of Your anointing (Isaiah 10:27).

Jesus, I acknowledge You as my Lord and Saviour. You died and rose again to heal my heart and deliver me from darkness. To set me free from the places of captivity Satan allocated to me and to release me from every power he has assigned to me for my destruction.

Lord, I repent for every sin I have knowingly and unknowingly participated in, which has opened the door for Satan to take hold of areas of my life. Holy Spirit, please bring to my mind every act for me to confess before Father God and Jesus now:

Father God, I ask You to forgive me for _____, _____, _____, _____.

I repent, I'm sorry for every involvement, participation, and action that violated my relationship with You. Thank You, Jesus, for Your blood shed for me that cleanses me from sin, allowing me access to Your abundant forgiveness, grace, and resurrection life.

Where there has been sin from previous generations that have gained power in my life, through my bloodline, please cleanse my bloodline now. On behalf of my ancestors, I repent for their involvement in *(wait for the Holy Spirit to bring specific things to your mind)* _____, which violated our family relationship with You. I call on the grace of Jesus to cancel the power of sin that has come through the family line of my ancestors. I declare I am a new creation through Christ Jesus, the old is gone, and the new is here (2 Corinthians 5:17). You are seated on high and Lord of my family. You are our dwelling place throughout all our generations (Psalm 90:1). From generation to generation, You are a strong tower, and the righteous run into it and are safe in Your protection (Proverbs 18:10).

Out of obedience to You, God, I choose to forgive those who harmed me. I don't justify their acts, I only release the right to hold onto bitterness, hurt, and offence. I forgive them and set them free from my heart. I release the hurt in my heart, and in doing so, I release the grip of hatred and anger that have lived with me. I breathe out all and every offence and breathe in the freedom of the Holy Spirit. Thank You, Lord.

A Prayer for Deliverance from Fear

I declare Jesus dismantled the rulers and authorities that have harassed me. He came to make a public spectacle of them, having triumphed over them through the cross (Colossians 2:15). Where fear has had licence in my life, driving my decisions, words, and relationships, I ask you to forgive me. I release all fear from my memories, my mind, my heart, and my body, including my stomach, shoulders, and neck. *(Take a moment to exhale and shake off any fear that may have been oppressing you; release all fear now.)* I speak healing to my brain, to my amygdala, and areas where fear has been stored in my mind and memories, and body, I pray for a total release right now, thank You, Lord. Where my brain has been triggered by old fear patterns, I ask for Your healing, Lord. For fear that has entered my body, brain, and memory through trauma and shock, I ask You to cancel these attachments and agreements with my body right now, Lord. All avenues through past trauma are closed right now. I thank You for healing every place of entry and closing off their access to fear right now. I cancel every assignment and curse that has been assigned to me because of generational fear through trauma. Thank You for drawing every trace of stored trauma out of my body now, Lord, as this has now been cancelled for my children and future children; they are set free from this cycle. The door to fear is now closed, and in every way, I am a new creation through Christ my Lord. I ask You for Your grace and confidence to trust in You with all my heart. I choose to live in the peace Jesus has given me (John 14:23).

I thank You, Lord, that You have created me to live an empowered life with You. To live in the authority Jesus gave me to tread on serpents and scorpions and over all the power of the enemy without harm (Luke 10:18–19). By faith, I declare every weapon and stronghold from the enemy that exults itself against the knowledge of You is cast down and demolished into the captivity of Christ in full obedience to You (2 Corinthians 10:4–5). I thank You that I am an overcomer through Christ our Lord (John 16:33). Thanks be to You, God, who gives me victory through our Lord Jesus Christ (1 Corinthians 15:57). I pray for Your daily grace to strengthen me against temptation, and deliver me from evil, Lord. The kingdom, the power, and the glory are Yours in my life today and tomorrow and forever and ever. Amen.

Prayer for Deliverance from Rejection

Lord, where my heart has lived in isolation, rejection, and loneliness, I renounce the grip rejection has gained in my heart. For every experience that has led me to believe I am separated from love, I renounce those lies.

(Confess out loud the lies you have believed and ask God to forgive you. Lies such as nobody likes me, I was not meant to be born, I am a burden, I am trouble. This is hard, but you are confessing these lies in faith and believing for God to break the power of these lies off your mind and heart.)

I thank You for cancelling agreements my brain and body have made with rejection that You would do a healing in the timeline of my life and place Your healing power on every event that disrupted my emotional and physical security. Every event that negatively affected my emotional development. By your grace, I ask You to mature and develop every area of development in me that has been stunted.

I ask You to restore balance to my brain, thought patterns, neurons, and connections. Where I have stressful, regretful, and traumatic thoughts that circulate around and around like a record repeating, I pray You would cancel the circuit. I ask that You reorder my memories, allowing encouraging and loving memories to be accessible and easily retrieved.

I thank You for Your overflowing love for me. That nothing can separate me from Your love. Where I have lived with an orphan spirit, I ask You to forgive me for being deceived and denying Your truth about me. I choose to live in the truth of my identity as a child of the Most High God, an heir through You, God (2 Timothy 3:16, Galatians 4:7). I thank You, Father God, that I can live in friendship with You (John 15:15). That the veil that separated us has been torn for us to live in close relationship through Christ. Thank You for loving and accepting me, for creating me, choosing me, and wanting me. That You are in my midst, to save me, You rejoice and sing over me with gladness, You quiet my heart with Your love, (Zephaniah 3:17). I receive Your abundant everlasting love and choose to carry it in my heart, body, and mind. Thank You, Lord.

Houses with Impure Spirits

At times, Christians may discover a new or existing home they are living in has paranormal activity occurring., or even an unexplainable oppressive atmosphere. Christians should not tolerate cohabiting with demonic spirits. Somewhere along the line, certain legal rights for demonic powers may have been acquired. Demons can gain access to premises through previous trauma in the house or on the land, which can include violent or abusive acts, occult practices, rituals, ceremonies, witchcraft, Ouija boards, and fortune-telling. This may have occurred before purchasing or renting the home. Allowing space for the demonic in our lives opens an unending invitation for unclean spirits to cultivate demonic powers in the environment. Not only can they disrupt and disturb relationships within the home, but they can also torment individuals with fear, confusion, and chaos.

In the following Scripture, Jesus explains we as Christians are like a house; when we are cleaned and delivered from the demonic without closing the door to occult activities, we invite even worse activity.

> When an impure spirit comes out of a person, it goes through arid places seeking rest and does not find it. Then it says, 'I will return to the house I left.' When it arrives, it finds the house unoccupied, swept clean, and put in order. Then it goes and takes with it seven other spirits more wicked than itself, and they go in and live there. And the final condition of that person is worse than the first. That is how it will be with this wicked generation. Matthew 12:43-45 NIV

This is why Christians need to repent of occult practices and live in obedience to God's instructions in the Bible. When this occurs, both our bodies, which are living temples of the Holy Spirit, and our physical homes will be protected from unclean spirits. The entry points and access are no longer available for demonic spirits to return. Instead, our environment and atmosphere become a safe place for t the Holy Spirit to dwell.

As a young child, my family lived in a home inhabited by a demonic spirit. We could hear footsteps running up and down the hallway, yet we couldn't actually see anything causing the noise. The presence would dash down the hallway and flush the toilet, stopping only when it reached a particular bedroom in the house—my childhood bedroom. We grew accustomed to it, unaware there was authority to change the situation. It simply was what it was.

Now armed with the tools to clear out demonic spirits, I have prayed with homeowners to remove them. One occasion comes to mind, when expelling a demonic spirit, the family dog yelped loudly at the spirit's exit. I've noticed over the years that if you pay attention, you may notice family pets are often very sensitive to the spirit life of a home and usually quite observant of what is happening.

If you're living in a home with demonic spirits, you might like to invite a member of a church prayer team to come to your home and pray with you or with a spouse or family member. Here is a suggested prayer that is powerful for closing the door to evil and ushering in the presence of the Holy Spirit.

Cleansing the Home from Impure Spirits

Note: Before beginning this prayer, gather a small amount of oil into a container you will use on some doorposts of your house during this prayer.

Lord, I confess You are Lord and Saviour of my life. As for me and my house, we will serve the Lord (Joshua 24:15). We dedicate this home to You, Lord, for our family to live a devoted life of faith, fellowship, and worship to You and You alone.

Lord, I repent for any and every occult symbol, item, game, movie, or media I have allowed into this home, either knowingly or unknowingly. I ask for Your forgiveness and turn away from allowing any further access to these influences. I also repent on behalf of previous owners for any occult activity in this home and property. We now dedicate our home to Christ to be an honouring dwelling place of Your Holy Spirit. From this day forward, help us be sensitive to anything that may disrupt Your atmosphere of peace. I claim Your rest and security within every room of our house right now.

You have given me authority to trample on snakes and scorpions and to overcome all the power of the enemy; as for me and my family, nothing will harm us (Luke 10:19). As I take authority over the atmosphere of our home, I do so with the full measure of authority in heaven and on earth that Jesus instated when He ascended into heaven (Matthew 28:18). I thank You that Your protection for our family is full and complete, for You are faithful, Lord, and You establish our family and guard us against the evil one (2 Thessalonians 3:3).

I now send out every spirit from this home that is not of You, Lord. By the authority of the name of Jesus Christ, every demonic spirit must leave right now. I resist the enemy and all demonic assignments and activity for this home, and they flee now. Every demonic presence is banished from our premises. From our home, our cars, and the entire property. Lord, I ask You to place angels to stand guard over every corner of our property and embrace Your Word that says we, Your people, will dwell in secure homes, in undisturbed places of rest (Isaiah 32:18).

Walk to the front door of your home. Place a small amount of oil on your finger and wipe it onto the top of your doorway, above your front door.

Lord, I place this oil here as a symbol of Your anointing and protection for our home. Our home is set aside and established in power and love from the Most High. I thank You that as we use this door, You watch over our coming and our going today and tomorrow (Psalm 121:8). I thank You that each time we come through our front door, our family will live in safety, quietly in our home. Here we find our rest (Isaiah 32:8). That You order Your angels to protect us wherever we go, in every room of our house (Psalm 91:11).

I proclaim the name of Jesus in this name and with it, the full authority of Christ instated in our presence. At the name of Jesus, every knee will bow, in heaven and on earth and under the earth, and every tongue acknowledge that Jesus Christ is Lord, to the glory of God the Father (Philippians 2:10–11). There is no other name under heaven which can save us (Acts 4:12).

Walk to the bedrooms of your home. Place oil at the top of each doorway. At the last bedroom, continue praying this prayer.

I thank You, Lord, that Your Word says we go to bed without fear, that we will lie down and sleep soundly (Proverbs 3:24). By Your grace, Lord, we live and move and have our being in You, living without fear, for You are with us. It is for total and complete freedom that Christ has set us free from the bondage of darkness. As a family, we choose to stand firm and not allow ourselves to be burdened by the slavery of fear or torment (Galatians 5:1). Instead, we willingly embrace Your peace as we rest our head on our pillows for in peace we will 'lie down and sleep, for you alone, Lord, make us dwell in safety' (Psalm 4:8).

Chapter 13

Freedom Prayers

Rebellion

Rebellion is seen in people who have a fear of being controlled. People operating in rebellion inherently do not trust the leadership structure in which they are positioned; they will likely fight to be independent and defy the instruction and guidance of their authority. Whether it's their parents, school, employer, church leaders, or others, they will separate themselves from any expectations of obedience to authority.

Fear can be a relevant factor here, specifically a fear of surrendering to authority and a deep desire to be autonomous and maintain control. This can result in a propensity to control the environment and control those around them. Manipulation may be a strong tool for those operating in rebellion. They will use it to exert control over their leaders, parents, peers, and friends. In a group activity, if they cannot be the leader and call the shots, they may choose not to be involved. Adults trying to lead a rebellious teen may find themselves accused and condemned, as the rebellious person may persist in trying to manipulate words, events, and circumstances to isolate authority from them.

The good news is rebellion is no match for our God, who overcame sin in the world by the work of Jesus' death and resurrection. Jesus came to set the captives free, and the person suffering from fear of being controlled can be radically set free and restored. God is sovereign in healing hearts. Every heart in each of our family members is so precious to Jesus, and He desires to heal and make us new creations in Christ Jesus. Our job is to trust Him and pray prayers of faith, with expectancy to see God do a deep work in our families.

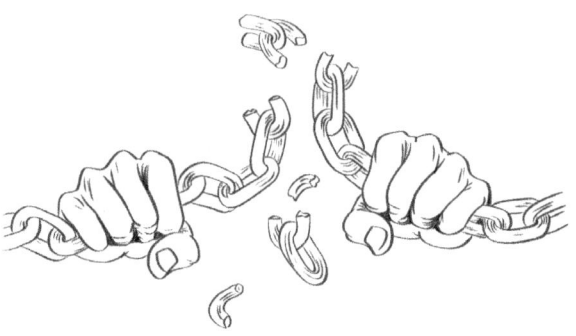

Many strong Christian leaders, both today and throughout history, have overcome the spirit of control and submitted their lives to God. They are powerful leaders with a tenacity to break new ground for God. As we pray for a loved one struggling with rebellion, pray out of a place of love, with a tenderness of heart and faith for God to heal their heart and set them free.

From Rebellion to Surrender—for a Loved One

Lord, we believe in Your promises despite our natural circumstances. Our family moves toward Your instruction. Lord, we pray to You with hope as we believe through the eyes of faith that You will continue to bless us as the offspring of Your promise to Abraham. Your Word says the seed of the righteous shall be delivered (Proverbs 11:21).

We commit to You now, our daughter/son (name), who is from Your seed, and we stand in Your truth and believe for their deliverance from the clutch of the enemy and the deceptive lure of this world. For Your Son, Jesus came to overcome the world.

Lord, I believe (name) is blessed by You. That Your power is fully released to work through them and You deliver them from the power of darkness. Where we, as parents, have focused on discipline more than on relationship, we are sorry. Please forgive us for the words spoken that have caused offence and formed a relationship of disrespect between us and our child. Guide us into a right relationship by the power of Your Holy Spirit, prompting us to where we need to apologise and how we can invest wisely in our relationship with our child.

Lord, I declare Your promises are higher than (name)'s physical reality and circumstances. Where rebellion has taken hold of their life, we pray for a breaking of these chains that have held them captive. We address the fear of being controlled and cancel its stronghold on them. Instead, we pray they will hold every thought captive to You (2 Corinthians 10:5) and prosper from fruit-bearing, Spirit-filled living. No longer being captive to fear. We ask that they have a softened heart with an openness and willingness to restore relationships with their family and to trust in You. Your Word says they are taught by You and great will be their peace (Isaiah 54:13). We break the power of the spirit of rebellion, and we cancel its effects on their life. We declare a separation from death and destruction, and every assignment, word, curse, and alignment with death. We ask that You add to (name) the length of their days, giving long life and peace (Romans 8:6). That all would be well with (name) as they dwell in safety with You. We believe You will supply every need of (name) according to Your riches in glory in Christ Jesus (Philippians 4:19).

Your Word says in Your hand, the king's heart is a stream of water You channel towards all who please you (Proverbs 21:1). If You can do this with powerful kings, then I believe that in Your hand (name)'s heart is fully transformed with rivers of living water channelled by You. That their heart would readily flow with the Holy Spirit, producing peace, love, faith, and every good fruit. We ask that You create in (name) a clean heart and renew a right spirit within them. Hold them close in Your presence with Your Holy Spirit and restore in them the joy of Your salvation to sustain in them a willing spirit (Psalm 51:10–12).

Lord, we receive Your Word that instructs us to be confident You who began a good work in (name) will carry it on to completion until the day of Christ Jesus (Philippians 1:6). We honour You for this truth You have revealed to us and believe the gifts, purposes, and plans You have created and begun in (name) would be fully fulfilled in them. That which You began in them would grow into maturity to bear a harvest of fruit for Your glory. That as You lead them out of darkness into Your light, their voice would proclaim that excellence of You who called them out of darkness and into Your marvellous light (1 Peter 2:9). Lord, You know the plans You have for (name), plans to prosper them and provide a hope and future (Jeremiah 29:11). So, we prophetically call Your plans into place. That chaos would be put in order. That Your peace would replace all fear. We call in opportunities for (name) that make way for Your plans for them to prosper. Stir hope in their heart of things You created for them long ago. May the purposes for their life become dreams in their heart, as longing fulfilled is like a tree of life (Proverbs 13:12).

Addiction

Addiction stems from a sense of emptiness. There is a place in our soul that only a connection with God can fill. When we don't find that intimacy with God, it leads to a longing that cannot be satisfied outside of God. Psalm 107:9 explains, 'He satisfies the longing soul, and the hungry soul he fills with good things' (ESV). God knows us so intimately that we discover our truest self through Him. We are created for a relationship with our creator! It's a two-way relationship, producing deep satisfaction and faithful friendship.

It's also true that we are shaped for relationships with others. Jesus instructed His disciples that the greatest command was to love God and love others. Without regular love and interaction with others, we are completely out of alignment with God's design for living. Not surprisingly, no substitute substance can fill a void shaped to be filled by God, friendship, and community.

And let us consider how we may spur one another toward love and good deeds, not giving up meeting together, as some are in the habit of doing, but encouraging one another—and all the more as you see the Day approaching.

Hebrews 10:24-25 NIV.

From Addiction to Connection: For a Loved One

We pray for (name) to align with Your truth, for grace to reign in their life through righteousness (Romans 5:17, 21). That the abundance of Your grace would abound in their living. Where (name) has been drawn into attachments of addiction, we ask in faith for You to make way for Your transforming power, which loosens the ties that hold him captive. That Your Spirit would prompt their heart to recognise their life is not working this way and You are their way maker (Isaiah 43:16), that they may sense You have more for them than this. That by Your mighty power at work within, you can do far more than they could ever dare to ask or dream of. Far beyond their highest prayers, desires, thoughts, or hopes (Ephesians 3:20). We ask that You humble their heart before You, that they would seek You with their whole heart and find You.

Lord, we pray for Your divine intervention for (name) to experience true connection with You. A deep and personal living relationship with You, their heavenly Father. That You would affirm Your relationship with them, reveal Yourself to them in ways that deeply reach and awaken their heart to You. I ask that You also bring them into strong, quality connections with others, allowing them to build solid friendships with people who will bring out the best in them. Please grant the discernment to reject the counsel of the wicked and turn down the company of mockers (Psalm 1:1–6). Instead, Lord, please plant them in a Christian community, with thriving fellowship and a deep sense of belonging. I pray they will be planted in the house of the Lord and be of great service to You and others.

Through the eyes of faith, we prophetically thank You that where death once reigned, (name) receives an abundance of righteousness with the gift of Your grace to reign in their life. We ask that they actively reject and relinquish the receiving of sin and death. Instead, we declare (name) lives in the reign of Your righteousness. We thank You that Your reign washes every area the enemy has gained. It drowns out all addiction, every sense of isolation, both from You and others, and all poverty and lack. It washes away all that was meant to destroy them. Thank You for a shift now, that the reign of our Lord Jesus Christ fills them with Your Spirit, wisdom, counsel, knowledge, and a deep reverence for You to live by each day. We declare the fruit of Your righteous reign in (name) is to live justly, with honesty and faithfulness to You and Your people. That their life would build a legacy of a peaceful and purposeful life, with love for You and others.

Regret

Living with the burden of regret can be one of the fastest and most effective ways for Satan to diminish your ability to lead a powerful and impactful life.

The nagging sense of failure and regret is the enemy's perfect tool, keeping you muted, inadequate, and unqualified to live out God's plan for your life. It can transform what should be a faith-filled life into a fear-filled existence.

So many people struggle to embrace the abundant fullness of Christ because they are entirely bound by self-condemnation.

David in the Bible, a man who personally experienced the favour and grace of God, fell into deep temptation and sin when he not only committed adultery with Bathsheba but also orchestrated her husband Uriah's death. This left him and his family vulnerable to the consequences of his actions. Yet despite the significant fallout from his sin, his renewed commitment to God allowed God's grace to bless him and the people of Judah through his leadership. David achieved several successes during his reign, including conquering Jerusalem and expanding the kingdom of Israel.

Our own sin can lead to relationship damage, financial strain, the burden of guilt, and emotional and physical issues. Yet, when we live a life submitted to Christ, it is not over until God says it's over. His gift of grace can turn the more dire consequences into beauty. God promises to grant beauty instead of ashes for those who mourn. The oil of joy instead of mourning, the garment of praise instead of the spirit of heaviness. He makes trees of righteousness as the planting of the Lord, that he will be glorified (Isaiah 61:3).

'And we know that for those who love God all things work together for good, for those who are called according to his purpose' (Romans 8:28 ESV).

Letting Go of Regret—For Self

Lord, may Your Holy Spirit help me as I pray this prayer. I choose not to live under the weight of regret. I ask You to forgive me for the choices and actions that have harmed my life both past and present. Touch my heart, Lord, take the weight of sorrow from me. I ask You to forgive me for every choice and action that has negatively affected others, including family members, friends, colleagues, neighbours, and strangers. I seek Your blessing, Your healing, and Your protection for each of these people.

I receive my freedom, for I believe Jesus came to set me free (John 8:36). Thank You for Your great love. Your compassion never fails. They are new every morning. Great is your faithfulness (Lamentations 3:22–23).

I receive Your truth that there is no condemnation for me, as I am in Christ Jesus. The law of the Spirit of life has set me free from sin and death (Romans 8:1–2).

I choose to set my mind on the things of the Spirit (Romans 8:5). Meditating on what is noble, just, pure, and praiseworthy (Philippians 4:8). Lord, please open my eyes to see things through Your perspective, for my heart and mind to realign with Your heart.

I believe You are my redeemer, and my future is in Your good hands. For You know the plans You have for me. Plans to prosper and not harm me. Plans to give me a hope and a future. Thank You that I live my life and future as a forgiven son/daughter.

Comparison

Comparing ourselves and what we have to others is the most foolish way to assess our worth and measure what we have received from God. What this comparison fails to do is see what God is doing beyond the surface. It does not factor in the deep work God is doing in and through us. The focus of comparison is purely superficial.

Theodore Roosevelt once said, 'Comparison is the thief of joy.' It can be so destructive that God even included it as the tenth commandment, 'You shall not covet your neighbour's house. You shall not covet your neighbour's wife, or his male or female servant, his ox or donkey, or anything that belongs to your neighbour' (Exodus 20:17 NIVUK). One reason God cares about this so much is it affects our hearts and turns our gratitude away from all that He has done for us.

It is not bad to choose to acquire things; it is just impossible to be captivated by worldly desire and remain devoted to God at the same time. We need to be disciplined about what we allow to consume our hearts, as God wants our whole hearts. Paul gives us the key to turning away from comparison. This key is gratitude! 'Give thanks in all circumstances; for this is God's will for you in Christ Jesus' (1 Thessalonians 5:18 NIV).

From Comparison to Contentment—For Self

Lord, I choose to willingly guard my heart. Where I am distracted by what others have, where my thoughts are ruminating on colleagues' work promotions, others' successes, and dreams being fulfilled, I am sorry. Where I have become fixated on other families having bigger or newer homes, cars, and holidays, sweeter children, and more attentive spouses, I ask for Your forgiveness. You alone are my portion and my cup; You make my lot secure. (Psalm 16:5). You make my life, home, family, future, hopes, and dreams secure.

I align with Your instructions to guard my heart with diligence and vigilance. Lifting my eyes to the mountains, for my help comes from You, Lord, the maker of heaven and earth, (Psalm 121:1–2). I ask that as the Holy Spirit dwells in me, my focus and mind would be set deeper into the things of the Spirit, to bear fruit for You.

I thank You that Jesus is interceding for me, and You have called me by name. May every heart's desire You have given me be fulfilled.

In faith, I believe Your Spirit guides these plans to fulfilment. I am confident the good work You have begun in me, You will perfect until the day of Jesus Christ (Philippians 1:6).

Grief

Grief has a unique way of gripping our souls. Its consequences can be surprising, with significant effects on our mood, energy, motivation, and relationships. While grieving a loved one is one of the most stressful experiences a person can endure, it is not the only source of grief. This is because grief extends beyond the loss of a loved one; it arises from loss in general.

The profound effects of grief often stem from our capacity to hope. The Bible says, 'Hope deferred makes the heart sick, but a longing fulfilled is a tree of life' (Proverbs 13:12 NIV). When we face the loss of our cherished dreams, it manifests in our heart and body as grief, felt like an illness within our heart, mind, and body. How often have we experienced or seen loved ones endure crushing loss, such as broken relationships, struggles with infertility, or a job that ended poorly, and so many other scenarios where dreams and hopes for the future were not realised and not grown into what was dreamed of? Something I've noticed over the years is grief often attaches itself to past grief. I've witnessed many people, including myself, have past experiences of loss stirred up when a new loss arises.

I was once working in a ministry that closed due to leadership changes. The weight of crushed hope affected me far more than the situation warranted. It took a seasoned minister with a gift in counselling to point out I was displaying symptoms of grief. After working through this with God, it became clear that although the grief was triggered by the closure of the ministry, the pain stemmed from a much deeper source. The impact of the loss was heightened by a previous loss from decades ago.

When we deal with grief that arises from deep tragedy, it can be tempting to blame others for the depth of pain we experience. It's human instinct to want to find someone to hold accountable. However, it's important to keep in perspective that the mistakes that contribute to tragedy can be amplified by the depth of emotion we feel. Life is complex; multiple people can contribute, so it's crucial to consider this to avoid placing sole responsibility for our grief on others, as our grief can be a multilayered emotion that includes a wide range of feelings.

From Grief to Hope—For Self

Thank You that You are near to the brokenhearted and You save those who are crushed in spirit (Psalm 34:18). My heart has been heavy, and my need for You is great. May the breath of Your Holy Spirit blow into my heart and spirit, reviving every part that has become crushed and bruised and broken.

Lord, there is pain in my loss; letting go grieves me deeply. My whole heart seeks You. I receive Your counsel. Even as I sleep, Lord, You minister to my heart (Psalm 16:7). I thank You that You bless and comfort me as I mourn (Matthew 5:4).

Where I have been dry and broken, crumbling like ashes, You give me the oil of joy for mourning. Where I have worn the spirit of heaviness, You give me a garment of praise to wear before You. You call me a tree of righteousness, planted by You to bring You glory (Isaiah 61:3). Thank You, Father.

Lord, I declare You are my God of hope, and You fill me with joy and peace as I believe and trust in You. I receive Your joy and peace to overflowing hope by the power of Your Holy Spirit (Romans 15:13). As I choose to place my hope in You and Your unfailing goodness, I receive Your strength as You renew me. I receive Your energy, strength, and power into my body as I soar on the wings of eagles. I can run without growing weary and walk without fainting (Isaiah 40:31). You bring health to my body and nourishment to my bones (Proverbs 3:8).

Thank You, Father, for making known to me the path of life. You fill me with joy in Your presence and share Your eternal pleasures with me (Psalm 16:11).

CHAPTER 14

Prayer

You may notice the practice of prayer has been highlighted throughout the book on multiple occasions. My intention is to help you be aware of the power of prayer and its vital place in our daily lives. However, rather than relying solely on the prayers of others or the prayers crafted in this book, my desire is that you will develop your confidence in praying your own personal prayers to God daily. In this chapter, I offer some specific insight into the 'how' and 'who' within our engagement of prayer.

How Does the Function of Prayer Work?

Here, I have outlined how each member of the Trinity engages with our prayers. It's helpful to understand how the Trinity works together to understand, sanctify, and answer our prayers. I have also included Satan's role concerning our prayers, as he actively tries to hinder them by being our accuser.

Holy Spirit

'And he who searches our hearts knows the mind of the Spirit, because the Spirit intercedes for God's people in accordance with the will of God' (Romans 8:27 NIV).

The Holy Spirit knows us so intimately that even the tone of our groans or utterings reveals a truth about our hearts and needs to Him. The Holy Spirit is not only the messenger from God to us, revealing truth, but also conveys our hearts to God. As we are temples for the Holy Spirit to dwell within, prayer acts as an invitation to activate the power of the Holy Spirit in our lives and circumstances.

The Holy Spirit is deeply relational, and our prayers usher in the assistance of the Holy Spirit during our weaknesses and struggles. 'In the same way, the Spirit helps us in our weakness. We do not know what we ought to pray for, but the Spirit himself intercedes for us through wordless groans' (Romans 8:26 NIV). We understand inviting the Holy Spirit into our prayer life brings freedom: 'Now the Lord is the Spirit, and where the Spirit of the Lord is, there is freedom' (2 Corinthians 3:17 NIV). During prayer, the Holy Spirit lightens our hearts, helping us to lay down the burdens we carry.

God

The apostle Paul taught that with prayer, through faith in Jesus, 'we may approach God with freedom and confidence' (Ephesians 3:12 NIV). We pray directly to God, but we do so with Jesus. Our prayers can take on a myriad of expressions and purposes; for instance, we might thank God, apologise for our mistakes, or ask Him to meet any and all needs.

We could be seeking wisdom, revelation, or insight on numerous matters. We have been granted the freedom and confidence to approach Him. 'Do not be anxious about anything, but in every situation, by prayer and petition, with thanksgiving, present your requests to God. And the peace of God, which transcends all understanding, will guard your hearts and your minds in Christ Jesus' (Philippians 4:6–7 NIV).

Satan

Satan and his demons keep an account of our words and actions that align with sin, and whenever they see an opportunity, Satan uses our words and sins as justification to accuse us.

'Then I heard a loud voice in heaven say, "Now have come the salvation and the power and the kingdom of our God, and the authority of his Messiah. For the accuser of our brothers and sisters, who accuses them before our God day and night, has been hurled down."' (Revelation 12:10 NIV).

Our words and actions create agreements and contracts with Satan and his powers. Satan can gain legal rights to people's lives based on these agreements and alliances with sin. He can even present these contracts and agreements to God as accusations, aiming to bind God's freedom for believers.

Jesus

The great news for believers is Jesus has been appointed as our mediator. He serves as a representative between believers and God. You may have noticed Christians conclude their prayers by saying, 'in Jesus' name, Amen.' This is because they acknowledge Jesus' appointed role in presenting their case to God.

Jesus, who is seated at the right hand of the Father in heaven, intercedes (prays) for us on our behalf and, in doing so, has the power to cancel every condemnation from Satan that is held against us. This enables God to close the case and cancel the penalty, which is separation from Him. 'Who then is the one who condemns? No one. Christ Jesus who died—more than that, who was raised to life—is at the right hand of God and is also interceding for us' (Romans 8:34 NIV). When we pray and repent, Jesus, the mediator, enables the accusations that Satan brings against us to be cancelled so that God calls us forgiven.

It is because of Jesus' blood, shed as payment for our sin, that Jesus can stand before God and celebrate our debt being paid. His blood speaks simply on our behalf. 'You have come to God, the Judge of all, to the spirits of the righteous made perfect, to Jesus the mediator of a new covenant, and to the sprinkled blood that speaks a better word than the blood of Abel' (Hebrews 12:23–24 NIV). His blood is the element that allows God's judgment to be in our favour every single time we have repented for our sin and have been represented by Jesus.

Our Example of Prayer: The Lord's Prayer

Jesus provided us with rich teaching on how to pray to God. He delivered a famous sermon on the Mount. During His message, His disciples asked Him how to pray. Jesus replied:

> This, then is how you should pray;
> 'Our Father in heaven,
> Hallowed be your name,
> Your kingdom come,
> Your will be done,
> On earth as it is in heaven.
> Give us today our daily bread.
> And forgive us our debts,

As we also have forgiven our debtors.
And lead us not into temptation,
But deliver us from the evil one.'
Matthew 6:9–13 NIV

What We Learn About Prayer from Jesus' Prayer

Our Father – The opening of this prayer teaches us to pray to God directly from the close relationship we share. It is an intimate acknowledgement of the position we hold in our relationship with God as His chosen children, with a Father who loves, creates, saves, directs, provides, speaks, listens, and heals.

In Heaven – Here, Jesus acknowledges God's position as being in heaven. Although God fills us and surrounds our lives with His Holy Spirit, He is also seated on the throne of heaven and still able to be omnipresent with us in every way. Seated in heaven, He is surrounded by all the resources of heaven; His desire is to bring His presence and spiritual resources to our reality on Earth. 'Praise be to the God and Father of our Lord Jesus Christ, who has blessed us in the heavenly realms with every spiritual blessing in Christ' (Ephesians 1:3 NIV).

Hallowed Be Your Name – An important part of prayer is acknowledging the holiness of God. This postures our hearts to worship Him through our prayers. Our worship blesses God and strengthens our faith in His power.

Your Kingdom Come, Your Will Be Done on Earth as It Is in Heaven – When we pray for His kingdom to come into our environment, with His will manifest in our family, work, church, community, and city, we surrender our plans to submit to His heavenly rule and reign. The kingdom of God is the realm God rules. This exists, of course, in heaven, but it can also be on Earth when we acknowledge and invite His Holy Spirit to fill our atmosphere. His desire is for us to pray for the glorious riches of Christ on Earth now; our prayer asks for a portion of heaven's reality, which is accessible to us now with the fullness to come in the future. God will 'bring unity to all things in heaven and on earth under Christ' (Ephesians 1:10 NIV).

Where Jesus is lifted up as Lord, the reign of God's kingdom is present. This doesn't have to be during a church service. You can experience the kingdom of God in your home and workplace by allowing Him to take the place of Lord. When this happens, the environment becomes subject to a heavenly measure of peace, power, joy, and the presence of God that changes situations and crowds out Satan and his powers.

Give Us Today Our Daily Bread – This part of Jesus' prayer reminds us that we can ask God each day to fulfil our daily needs and provide for us through our heavenly Father. Our requests are not limited to just bread; they can encompass a wide range of needs. We may ask for work, positioning, opportunities, healing, relationships, and peace. Anything we require should be brought before our Father God in faith. Jesus used the example of bread to teach us to pray daily for our needs. He doesn't instruct us to beg God but simply to ask in faith for our needs to be met. During His ministry, Jesus supernaturally multiplied bread to feed thousands, demonstrating God's power of provision and His value for fellowship. The example of bread has several biblical contexts. Here are a few:

Bread to Eat

- **For our physical nourishment.** 'I have been young, and now am old, yet I have not seen the righteous forsaken or his children begging for bread' (Psalm 37:25 ESV).

- **For our spiritual nourishment.** 'Jesus said to them, "I am the bread of life; whoever comes to me shall not hunger, and whoever believes in me shall never thirst"' (John 6:35 ESV).

- Breaking Bread for Fellowship

- **Fellowship with others** – Bread serves as a symbol of our daily fellowship with other believers. 'They devoted themselves to the apostles' teaching and to the fellowship, to the breaking of bread and to prayer' (Acts 2:42 NIV).

- **Fellowship with Christ** – Now that Jesus has died and risen to life, it symbolises our reconciliation through Him. 'And he took the bread, and when he had given thanks, he broke it and gave it to them, saying, "This is my body, which is given for you. Do this in remembrance of me"' (Luke 22:19 ESV).

And Forgive Us Our Debts. In the Bible, David, the psalmist, poet, musician, king of Israel, and shepherd, understood intimately what it meant to be forgiven by God, as his sin significantly impacted himself, his family, and the kingdom of Israel. He writes from a personal revelation of God's forgiveness for us, His people. 'As far as the east is from the west, so far has he removed our transgressions from us' (Psalm 103:12 NIV). Living with our sin removed allows us to dwell in the righteousness of Christ.

In the Lord's Prayer, with the line 'forgive us our debts,' Jesus teaches us to seek God and ask Him for His vast forgiveness, for He knows we live in a world where we will need to seek His forgiveness as we strive to walk in the purity and righteousness of Christ. It's not if we sin; it's when we sin, 'for all have sinned and fall short of the glory of God' (Romans 3:23 ESV). This forgiveness is so powerful and complete that the prophet Isaiah shared that when God chooses not to remember our sins, it is final: 'I, even I, am he who blots out your transgressions, for my own sake, and remembers your sins no more' (Isaiah 43:25 NIV). This radical level of undeserved forgiveness comes from God's grace to us, allowing us to live in relationship and freedom with Him.

As We Also Have Forgiven Our Debtors – While our forgiveness is as wide as the north is from the west, Jesus teaches that a requirement comes with it. The forgiveness we accept from God must have a flow-on effect, extending to others. Jesus explained it like this, 'For if you forgive other people when they sin against you, your heavenly Father will also forgive you. But if you do not forgive others their sins, your Father will not forgive your sins' (Matthew 6:14–15 NIV). Are we hearing this right? Yes, we are. If we are holding a grudge against others, it blocks the flow of Jesus forgiving us. I like to think of forgiveness as a circle of fiery love. It flows from God, through Jesus, then through us, and continues to those who wrong us, and Jesus receives it back through Him and turns the ashes into beauty. If we fail to do our part, which is to forgive, then the path is short-circuited, disrupting the flow of our forgiveness being received. The grace offered to us is immensely extensive, but to whom much is given, much is required.

If we hold onto bitterness, the ashes linger in our soul, creating a toxic poison that affects our physical and mental health as well as our spirit. It is possible to forgive terrible acts, even when the person seems undeserving. God's grace was given to us when we didn't deserve it. When we forgive, we do not condone what happened; we simply choose to hand it over to God, the righteous Judge. When we forgive and offer our ashes to God, He transforms them into beauty. He promises to 'provide for those who grieve in Zion—to bestow on them a crown of beauty instead of ashes, the oil of joy instead of mourning, and a garment of praise instead of a spirit of despair. They will be called oaks of righteousness, a planting of the Lord for the display of his splendour' (Isaiah 61:3 NIV).

And Lead Us Not into Temptation – People engage in certain practices that lead them directly into temptation. Most often, this is driven by our emotions, as they can serve as a powerful magnet unless we are deliberate in resisting such occurrences. We require wisdom and discernment to identify these specific activities. Additionally, we need the insight to observe the patterns of behaviour that lead us to sin. We can pray and ask God to allow the Holy Spirit to open our eyes to these matters.

For example, I know a man who wanted to be free from the bondage of pornography, so he stopped using the internet at home until the pattern of behaviour was broken. His temptation was removed, and as a result, his bondage to that sin was lifted. Personally, I know murder documentaries created a darkness in my soul and affected my heart. By guarding my heart against these documentaries, I move away from fear and depression. Consequently, I choose to refrain from watching them. Whatever type of sin may tempt you, the discipline of working alongside the Holy Spirit to resist Satan's attempts to lure us is crucial. We are more than capable of resisting Satan, and the Bible teaches us this with the passage, 'Submit yourselves, then, to God. Resist the devil, and he will flee from you' (James 4:7). We become less susceptible to temptation when we are strong in spirit. When we build our faith by staying close to God through prayer, reading the Bible, and fellowshipping with other believers, we become significantly less vulnerable to sin and much stronger in resisting temptation.

Even before Jesus taught His disciples the Lord's Prayer, God's people had learned quite a bit about sin through stories of many individuals in Scripture, including Adam and Eve, Noah's generation, David, and numerous others. Many lessons can be drawn regarding how each person was tempted, why they were vulnerable to temptation, how they sinned, and what insights can be gleaned about the consequences of their actions. We can learn from the story of Adam and Eve's sons, Cain and Abel. Right before Cain killed Abel, God said these words to him, knowing his heart was filled with jealousy: 'If you do what is right, will you not be accepted? But if you do not do what is right, sin is crouching at your door; it desires to have you, but you must rule over it' (Genesis 4:7 NIV).

But Deliver Us from the Evil One. This prayer concludes with a plea to God for protection against Satan and his powers. We are to pray in faith that God, as the victor over all, will shield us from becoming victims of the schemes of evil. In faith, we live with the prayer and belief that God delivers, saves, rescues, and protects us from evil.

God doesn't leave us defenceless against Satan; instead, He equips us with the full armour of God. He knows we will face battles and need complete protection to be saved and delivered from the evil one. This is why we have pieces of armour for our entire selves to be protected. With guarding our hearts, which is essential for survival, the shield of faith becomes a crucial piece of armour.

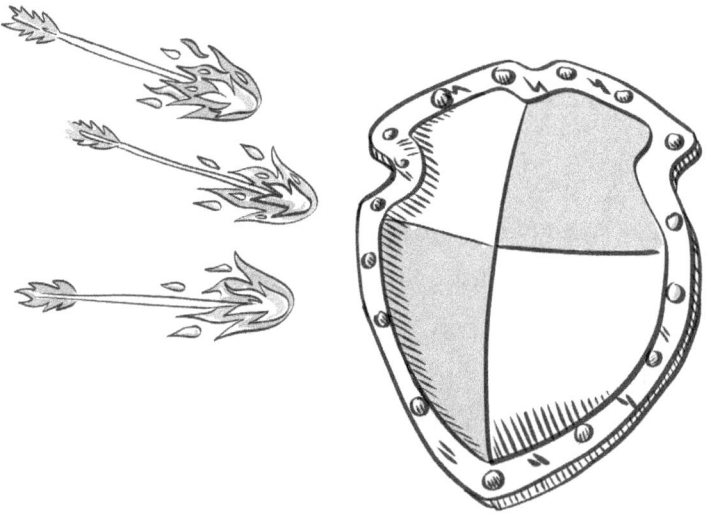

Paul explains it like this, 'In all circumstances take up the shield of faith, with which you can extinguish all the flaming darts of the evil one' (Ephesians 6:16 ESV). Do you notice how he says 'in all circumstances' and this will extinguish 'all' the flaming arrows? This 'all' allows us to have an 'all-consuming' faith that with God, we are truly protected.

It's interesting to know a little bit about the context of the kind of shield Paul was referring to in his letter to the Ephesian church. Those hearing his message were very familiar with a Roman shield, which was made of layers of heavy wood and covered with a leather canvas. Roman soldiers needed to oil the leather daily to keep it supple. Before each battle, they also soaked the leather with water to make the shield resistant to fire and to extinguish any flames that came against them.[2] The spiritual application of this analogy is our faith in God acts as a shield we hold over our hearts in faith. Our shield is oiled daily by the empowerment we receive from the Holy Spirit during prayer. The water applied before battle represents the cleansing and renewal of the Holy Spirit, as we believe in faith that we can trust God.

I think it's important that we don't remain in a constant state of fight. But as part of God's army, we can take our positions of 'abide' to stand strong in faith and His protection. To abide in trust means to simply hand the battle over to Him and maintain faith that He is victorious. We allow Him to be our dwelling place as we abide in His faithfulness. He is our shield and rampart within which we can find refuge. 'He will cover you with his feathers, and under his wings you will find refuge; his faithfulness will be your shield and rampart' (Psalm 91:4 NIV). It involves being faithful and rooted in God's Holy Spirit, which is His river of life and provides us with the strength we need to endure through evil, unrest, turmoil, and trouble. King David described it like this, 'Blessed is the one who does not walk in step with the wicked or stand in the way that sinners take or sit in the company of mockers, but whose delight is in the law of the Lord, and who meditates on his law day and night. That person is like a tree planted by streams of water, which yields its fruit in season and whose leaf does not wither—whatever they do prospers' (Psalm 1:1–3 NIV).

Chapter 15

Praying for God's Will in Our Lives

God has set a purpose for believers that He equips us for, according to the counsel of His will, which is in our hearts and expressed through the Holy Spirit's guidance. The Holy Spirit intercedes for us before God. 'In him we were also chosen, having been predestined according to the plan of him who works out everything in conformity with the purpose of his will' (Ephesians 1:11 NIV). While God does not reveal what He has done from beginning to end, He allows us to know in our hearts that we are part of an eternal plan. We inherently understand we are created with a purpose, and God has established a purpose for us in His kingdom.

Jesus Lived in the Will of the Father

Jesus knew His Father God had a prechosen eternal plan to which He was willing to submit. Jesus even spoke these words, 'Then I said, "Here I am—it is written about me in the scroll—I have come to do your will, my God"' (Hebrews 10:7 NIV). Jesus was able to submit to God's plan and actively prayed in alignment with it. As Jesus discerned God's will for Him as the sacrificial Lamb, He understood the suffering; however, out of love for God and for us, He was still willing to be used by God. This is how He prayed: 'He went away a second time and prayed, "My Father, if it is not possible for this cup to be taken away unless I drink it, may your will be done"' (Matthew 26:42 NIV).

Jesus' submission to God was vital for His purpose as Saviour and position, which was allocated by God to be seated in heavenly places at the right hand of the Father. God chose to position Jesus 'far above all rule and authority, power and dominion, and every name that is invoked, not only in the present age but also in the one to come. And God placed all things under his feet and appointed him to be head over everything for the church, which is his body, the fullness of him who fills everything in every way' (Ephesians 1:21–23 NIV).

Discerning His Will for Our Calling

When reflecting on our calling, we should consider:

Is there a grace in my life that not everyone possesses? For instance, do I have a strong ability to remember people's names and stories? Do I have a unique talent for leadership? Am I capable of managing money in a way that enhances finances? Can I organise things in a manner that often draws comments from others? Am I particularly effective in crises? Do people frequently seek my advice? Take note of the natural graces that God has bestowed upon you.

What gives me deep satisfaction and makes me feel fulfilled? It's valuable to ask yourself what delighted your heart when you were younger. This reflection can help you understand the purpose for which God crafted you. Our family has a photo that captures my husband, Phil, alongside his brother as young boys sitting on the floor, surrounded by a pile of screws, bolts, and bits. They had taken apart some of the family's electrical items and were attempting to reassemble them. Thankfully, their mother had the wisdom to allow this, despite the uncertainty and inconvenience. Both boys eventually became engineers, with my husband working as an electrical engineer. This has always been their true passion and calling. They both carry a strong evangelistic heart and gifting within their workplaces. God needs Christians everywhere.

What unique gifts of the Holy Spirit has God given me?
In one of his letters to the church of Corinth, the apostle Paul discusses the gifts from the Holy Spirit with new Christians. He says, 'Brothers and sisters, I want you to know about the gifts of the Holy Spirit' (1 Corinthians 12:1 NIRV). Whenever Paul says 'Brothers and sisters,' he is addressing Christians. Here we learn the gifts of the Holy Spirit are bestowed upon Christians when we have received the empowerment of the Holy Spirit. Paul continues,

The Holy Spirit is given to each of us in a special way. That is for the good of all. To some people, the Spirit gives a message of wisdom. To others, the same Spirit gives a message of knowledge. To others, the same Spirit gives faith. To others, that one Spirit gives gifts of healing. To others, He gives the power to perform miracles. To others, He gives the ability to prophesy. To others, He gives the ability to discern spirits. To others, He gives the ability to speak in different kinds of languages they had not known before. And to still others, He gives the ability to explain what was said in those languages. All the gifts are produced by one and the same Spirit. He gives gifts to each person, just as He decides.

1 Corinthians 12:7–11 NIRV

At first glance, it is tempting to think these gifts are only useful if you are working in Christian ministry as a minister. However, many of these gifts are being exercised by Christians in a wide variety of contexts. Would you choose a surgeon gifted with wisdom? Or a CEO with a gift of faith who can move mountains? How about a psychologist operating in the gift of discernment who, with the Holy Spirit, can be a vital instrument of God's healing? God needs Christians in every walk and every sector of life, and He equips us for the calling He places on our lives.

Are there areas where I sense God is leading me? Often, this can be through Bible verses or circumstances far too obscure to be mere coincidence. It may also involve multiple people sharing the same idea within a short time frame. At times, trusted leaders possess the wisdom to guide us into different opportunities that develop us and help lead us to our calling, while also being careful to use our own discernment. The uniqueness and variety of ways He prompts us are truly endless.

There have been a few times in my life when God has shown me the next steps through dreams. I remember receiving a dream from the Holy Spirit. In my dream, God told me to go to a particular college, which I wasn't familiar with. There was such a strong emotion in my dream where I felt God wanting me to trust Him. This strong stirring stayed with me the next morning, so I searched online for the college. I was very shocked to discover it was a Bible college. Although I ended up waiting two years before realising God was confirming this, the dream became influential in my decision to enrol in the Bible college. Amazingly, one week after enrolling, I was contacted by a teacher at a school who asked me to consider teaching Biblical Studies on staff, which would involve teaching three hundred students per fortnight. This role ultimately led to many ministry opportunities. It was very much a step of obedience leading to the next step, with God unravelling my path, calling me one step at a time.

Is there a longing in my heart that just won't go away? Often, we overlook the yearning in our hearts because it doesn't make sense to us. Or we can't quite see how that could be profitable or sustainable. But God wants us to have childlike faith and trust Him, as He isn't restricted by the barriers and limitations we perceive.

God hears, He answers, and He equips us for His will.

Moses was a man who despised the injustice his people were facing in Egypt. He detested it so much that he ended up murdering an oppressor. His heart yearned for freedom for his people. When God called him to help bring that freedom, he became hindered by his limited speech, as he suffered from a speech impediment. God overcame this obstacle by providing him with his brother Aaron as a spokesperson. He also equipped Moses with every resource needed along the journey, even to the point of parting the Red Sea. Our barriers are nothing to God. We need to move forward in confidence, knowing He hears, answers, and prepares us for the tasks we undertake in faith to fulfil His will for our lives.

God knows the plans He has for us, both from a big-picture perspective and in our daily lives. "'For I know the plans I have for you,' declares the Lord, 'plans to prosper you and not to harm you, plans to give you hope and a future'" (Jeremiah 29:11 NIV).

As we sense God's purpose in our hearts, we pray into it. We must believe He hears us and expect He will answer our prayers and equip us to fulfill our purpose within His kingdom. In fact, we can have confidence to pray for anything that aligns with God's Scripture and God's truth. We can confidently declare His Word because He desires for us to ask for anything according to His will. John the evangelist in the Bible teaches us, 'I write these things to you who believe in the name of the Son of God so that you may know that you have eternal life. This is the confidence we have in approaching God: that if we ask anything according to His will, He hears us. And if we know that He hears us whatever we ask — we know that we have what we asked of Him' (1 John 5:13–16 NIV). When we act in faith according to what we believe God purposed for us to do, God truly does provide the details that enable us to do His work.

The reward of submitting to God's will grants us the blessing of living out His will on earth. It embodies a life of faith and acknowledges the activity of God as He provides for our callings. However, there is also an eternal blessing and reward in heaven that is given to us: 'Rejoice and be glad, because great is your reward in heaven, for in the same way they persecuted the prophets who were before you' (Matthew 5:12 NIV). Jesus spoke about this matter, explaining that when we need to give things up to do His will, we receive one hundred times more when we get to heaven. '"Truly I tell you," Jesus replied, "no one who has left home or brothers or sisters or mother or father or children or fields for me and the gospel will fail to receive a hundred times as much in this present age: homes, brothers, sisters, mothers, children and fields—along with persecutions—and in the age to come eternal life" (Mark 10:29–30 NIV). Can you imagine how missionaries must feel going to unreached nations to share the gospel, leaving behind the comforts of family relationships and homes, and going into the unknown? The cost would come with an earthly reward, witnessing the fruit of their message change lives, but also a reward in heaven.

Chapter 16

Prayers for Others

Here is a range of prayers to help you declare in bold, faith-filled belief. As you pray, let your faith in God rise above any uncertainty you're facing. Where your best efforts fall short, that's where faith steps in, and that's where God loves to show His glory in your family and circumstances. Align your faith with God's promises, for He is a limitless God who can do immeasurably more than we could ever hope or imagine.

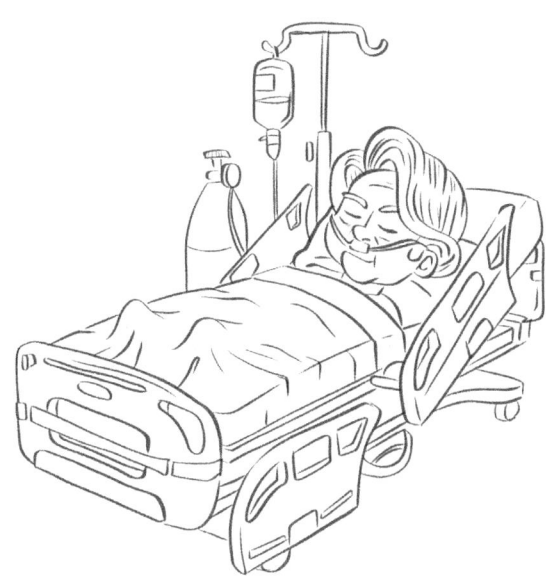

A Prayer of Protection

Lord, I surrender (name) to You today with trust and belief that there is no greater shelter of protection than You. I thank You for Your protection from accidents, illness, and evil intent. That Your Holy Spirit prompts them at all times, giving direction, solutions, and wisdom at every hour of the day and night. I declare that whenever they turn to the right or the left, their ears will hear Your voice behind them saying, 'This is the way; walk in it' (Isaiah 30:21 NIV). Thank You for every angel You order to protect all members of our family wherever they go today (Psalm 91:11). That whenever (name) will call to You in trouble, You will answer them, rescue, and honour them (Psalm 91:15). I thank You for Your promise to cover and provide refuge, that Your faithfulness to them would be a shield from the enemy, offering them a safe place of protection (91:4–7). I ask that You reassure their heart of Your unfailing safeguarding so that they would do as You continually encourage and to live life without fear, for they are with You. To live without worry of the enemy's schemes, but instead believe in their hearts that You are enough. I thank You for Your helmet of salvation firmly placed on (name)'s head. To protect their mind from the schemes of the enemy and engage their thoughts with all hope and endurance. I declare the mind of Christ for them. To stand against the forces of evil in heavenly places. (name) is seated with Christ in heavenly realms (Ephesians 2:6), sharing with Him in authority, identity, and victory by your saving grace, Lord.

A Prayer for Someone Sick

I thank You, Lord, that You sustain (name) in their illness, that You would restore them to full health (Psalm 41:3). I believe (name) receives their healing for the kingdom of God has come near to them (Luke 10:9).

I pray for (name) with the authority of Jesus to heal every disease and affliction they are facing today. Your Word says the blood of Jesus speaks for them (Hebrews 12:24), the blood of Jesus releases them from the captivity of sickness. Thank You for being our great physician who came to rescue the sick and call righteousness (Luke 5:31–32). I look to Jesus, the founder and perfecter of my faith, who endured the cross with joy for my freedom (Hebrews 12:1–3).

(name) receives Your glorious riches from the abundance of You, their heavenly Father, every need is met. Physically, mentally, emotionally, and spiritually, You have powerfully broken through to lavish them with generous provision. Your glory, power, and presence touch their body and mind right now. Every organ, limb, and system in their body is deeply soaked with the transformative presence and power of You, their heavenly Father. Lord, You make the riches of Your glory known to them with mercy, which You prepared in advance for Your glory (Romans 9:23). We thank You. Lord, that You cover (name) with Your feathers and under Your wings, where they find refuge. Your faithfulness is their shield and rampart, for You are their safe place (Psalm 91:4).

A Prayer for Direction

Lord, I pray for (name). I thank You that You hold them in Your right hand, and their future is secure with You. I ask that (name) would truly seek You with their whole heart, as Your Word promised those who seek You with their whole hearts will find You (Jeremiah 29:13). I pray that You would be first and foremost in every decision they make about their life and future. That as they search out Your future and direction, You would be their true north, showing the way to walk and the way to go.

I thank You for the patience from Your Holy Spirit to be poured out to them to wait on You, not being distracted from Your direction for the next steps. That (name) would have the courage to wait and believe You have plans and a future filled with hope and promise (Psalm 27:14). Your plans will prosper and never harm them (Jeremiah 29:11). Lord, I believe You reveal Your calling to Your children and Your sheep hear Your voice (John 10:27–28). That (Name) hears Your voice, that Your Holy Spirit moves their heart to respond to You, ushering in the direction You have already planned for them. Thank You for the victorious plans You placed in (name)'s heart.

May they never be lured by the plans of the enemy or the ways of the world. But instead commit every way to You, trust in You and see You give them the desires in their heart (Psalm 37:4). As they are presented with different choices and opportunities, I ask that in every way they would seek first Your kingdom and Your righteousness, living as salt and light to the world, with mercy, purity of heart. May they receive You, Lord, and live as Your child. (Matthew 5 and 6:1).

May Your Word be a constant lamp to their feet, lighting up Your direction for them, (Psalm 119:105). Showing them the path of righteousness and specific direction. Illuminate the path that leads them to diligently study Your Word, always choosing to travel the highway of holiness that leads to an everlasting relationship with You.

A Prayer for Sound Sleep

Jesus, I thank You that You are Lord of our family and Lord of our home. I stand in truth and take authority over the atmosphere of our property, home, and every room of our house. Within the space of our bedrooms, Lord, Your peace rests upon us. Your peace rests upon our minds. Your kingdom is near, and the atmosphere of heaven is all around us. Tonight, as we lie down and sleep, we willingly embrace Your peace as we rest our heads on our pillows, for You alone make us dwell in safety (Psalm 4:8).

We will not fear the terror of the night (Psalm 91:5) for You, Lord, are our deliverer, our shield, and our refuge (2 Samuel 22:2–3). You keep us safe in the shelter of Your dwelling and hide us in the shelter of Your tent (Psalm 27:5). Thank You, Lord, that You are in our midst as we lie in our beds tonight. You are the God who saves, who rejoices over us with You. We rest in Your love and joy as You sing over us (Zephaniah 3:17).

Prayer for the Salvation of a Loved One

Lord, I thank You for Your steadfast Lordship, Your sovereign plan, and Your redemptive love. We acknowledge You as the Alpha and Omega, the First and the Last, the Beginning and the End (Revelation 22:13). You are the orchestra and perfecter of our faith (Hebrews 12:2).

Lord, I commit (name) to You. Thank You for their life, purpose, and future. Thank You for lovingly creating (name) in Your image with a purpose and a plan for their life.

Thank You for loving (name) so much that You gave Your Son Jesus, so that (name) can believe in You and not perish but have eternal life (John 3:16). That You have not come to condemn (name) but to save them. Lord, remind them of Your Word that says You have revealed Yourself to those who did not ask for You and that You were found by those who did not seek You (Isaiah 65:1). I ask that *You* convict (name)'s heart of their need for You. That they would repent of doing life independently from You, for being seduced and deceived by the world and its many temptations. That they would confess all regret, and You would incline Your ear and heart to them.

By Your Spirit that You draw (name) into a relationship with You. Thank You for Your promise that as (name) draws near to You, You would draw near to them (James 4:8). I ask that You send Your Spirit to invite (name) into unique personal encounters that will minister deeply to both heart and spirit. Where there has been disappointment or doubt that has distracted (name) from a relationship with You in the past, I break the power of those experiences and pray for a release of Your healing and power into those places of their heart, mind, and spirit.

I believe in faith that (name) will declare with their mouth and believe in their heart that Jesus Christ is Lord, and God raised Jesus from the dead. That You would justify (name) as their heart goes deep in its belief, and their lips will profess faith in You. That (name) who calls on the name of the Lord will be saved (Romans 10:8–13).

Lord, I ask You to surround (name) with godly people. In their school, work, sporting teams, groups, and neighbours. For every walk of life, I ask that You put discerning, Spirit-filled people all around. Give these people a heart to invest in (name) to speak words of truth, life, hope, correction, encouragement, and wisdom. Lord, Your Word says that whoever walks with the wise becomes wise (Proverbs 13:20), so I ask that they grow in wisdom and knowledge and favour with You and Your people. (Luke 2:52). I declare that (Name) is more than a conqueror through Christ our Lord (Romans 8:37).

May (name) be discipled in Your Word and grow to become a disciple maker. Like Daniel in his obedience to you and like Joshua in his courage and leadership. That they would be planted in the house of the Lord, steadfast in the church, and pillars in the community. May they serve the vulnerable and be a deep source of wisdom for many. Have Your way, Lord, You are the way maker and promise keeper. Thank You. We pray in faith because You are able. You do exceedingly and abundantly above all that we can ask or think, according to the power that works in (name) (Ephesians 3:20). In Jesus' name, Amen.

Continue in Love

My prayers are for you, each reader. May you continue to grow in love. Keeping Jesus' words close to your heart.

"'Love the Lord your God with all your heart, with all your soul, and with all your mind," and "Love your neighbor as yourself'" (Mark 12:30–31). May this love be the foundation for each prayer that you pray. May His blessing rest upon you and your families.

About the Author

Kathleen is an Australian Christian minister, chaplain, and writer with a strong background in prayer ministry, cross-cultural mission work, preaching, and pastoral care. She lives in a coastal town in Melbourne, Australia, with her husband and three young adult children. Kathleen has been ministering to children and families for twenty-six years. She is passionate about empowering families through prayer and loves equipping them with the gospel.

Kathleen welcomes thoughtful connection with her readers. Whether you have a question, a reflection, or simply want to share your growth and journey. You can reach her directly by email at: **author.kvergers@gmail.com**

About the Illustrator

Paul Joy is a Melbourne-based artist whose hand-drawn visuals bring clarity and insight to complex ideas. A skilled sketchnoter, calligrapher, and illustrator, he integrates visual storytelling into his work as a preacher, speaker, and educator. Paul is an ordained minister and currently serves as a School Chaplain and Visual Art teacher. He also leads online drawing workshops and has illustrated a range of publications in both Australia and the United States. Paul lives with his wife and three children in Melbourne.

To see more of Paul's work or get in touch, visit www.handdrawntoday.com or email **handdrawntoday@gmail.com**.

Notes

1   Francis, Brown, S. R. Driver, and Charles A. Briggs. *A Hebrew and English Lexicon of the Old Testament* (Oxford: Clarendon Press, 1906).

2   Rick Renner, *How to Maintain Your Shield of Faith: Ancient Roman Secrets Revealed*, Harrison House, 2023, p. X

www.ingramcontent.com/pod-product-compliance
Lightning Source LLC
Chambersburg PA
CBHW071242070526
44583CB00017B/2301